COOKING WITH
CHILIES

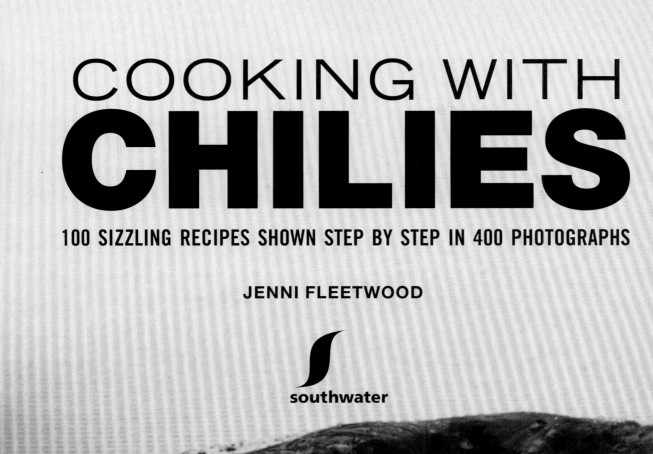

COOKING WITH
CHILIES

100 SIZZLING RECIPES SHOWN STEP BY STEP IN 400 PHOTOGRAPHS

JENNI FLEETWOOD

southwater

This edition is published by Southwater, an imprint of Anness Publishing Ltd,
Hermes House, 88–89 Blackfriars Road, London SE1 8HA; tel. 020 7401 2077; fax 020 7633 9499
www.southwaterbooks.com; www.annesspublishing.com

If you like the images in this book and would like to investigate using them for publishing, promotions or advertising,
please visit our website www.practicalpictures.com for more information.

UK agent: The Manning Partnership Ltd;
tel. 01225 478444; fax 01225 478440;
sales@manning-partnership.co.uk
UK distributor: Grantham Book Services Ltd;
tel. 01476 541080; fax 01476 541061;
orders@gbs.tbs-ltd.co.uk
North American agent/distributor: National Book Network;
tel. 301 459 3366; fax 301 429 5746;
www.nbnbooks.com
Australian agent/distributor: Pan Macmillan Australia;
tel. 1300 135 113; fax 1300 135 103;
customer.service@macmillan.com.au
New Zealand agent/distributor: David Bateman Ltd;
tel. (09) 415 7664; fax (09) 415 8892

Publisher: Joanna Lorenz
Managing Editor: Linda Fraser
Editor: Jennifer Schofield
Production Controller: Pirong Wang
Editorial Reader: Penelope Goodare
Designer: Nigel Partridge
Typesetters: Diane Pullen and Jonathan Harley
Recipes contributed by: Catherine Atkinson, Alex Barker, Angela Boggiano, Carla Capalbo, Kit Chan, Maxine Clark, Jacqueline Clarke,
Trish Davies, Patrizia Diemling, Matthew Drennan, Tessa Evelegh, Silvano Franco, Shirley Gill, Brian Glover, Rosamund Grant,
Nicola Graimes, Deh-Ta Hsuing, Shehzad Husain, Christine Ingram, Manisha Kanani, Lucy Knox, Lesley Mackley,
Sally Mansfield, Norma Miller, Jane Milton, Sallie Morris, Annie Nichols,
Jennie Shapter, Liz Trigg, Laura Washburn, Jeni Wright
Photography: Karl Adamson, Edward Allwright, Micki Dowie, James Duncan, Ian Garlick,
Michelle Garrett, Amanda Heywood, Ferguson Hill, Janine Hosegood, David Jordan,
Dave King, William Lingwood, Patrick McLeavey, Steve Moss,
Thomas Odulate, Craig Robertson, Simon Smith, Sam Stowell

ETHICAL TRADING POLICY

Because of our ongoing ecological investment programme, you, as our customer, can have the pleasure and reassurance of knowing that
a tree is being cultivated on your behalf to naturally replace the materials used to make the book you are holding. For further information
about this scheme, go to www.annesspublishing.com/trees If you like the images in this book and would like to investigate using
them for publishing, promotions or advertising, please visit our website www.practicalpictures.com for more information.

Previously published as *Turn Up The Heat*

NOTES

Bracketed terms are intended for American readers.
For all recipes, quantities are given in both metric and imperial measures and, where appropriate,
measures are also given in standard cups and spoons. Follow one set, but not a mixture,
because they are not interchangeable.
Standard spoon and cup measures are level. 1 tsp = 5ml, 1 tbsp = 15ml, 1 cup = 250ml/8fl oz
Australian standard tablespoons are 20ml. Australian readers should use 3 tsp in place of
1 tbsp for measuring small quantities of gelatine, flour, salt etc.
American pints are 16fl oz/2 cups. American readers should use 20fl oz/2.5 cups in place of 1 pint when measuring liquids.
Electric oven temperatures in this book are for conventional ovens. When using a fan oven, the temperature will probably need to be reduced
by about 10–20°C/20–40°F. Since ovens vary, you should check with your manufacturer's instruction book for guidance.
Medium (US large) eggs are used unless otherwise stated.

Main front cover image shows Spicy Meatballs, for recipe – see page 92.

PUBLISHER'S NOTE

CONTENTS

INTRODUCTION

There's a ring of fire encircling the globe, and it has nothing to do with volcanic activity. This is fire we're very much in favour of: the warmth that comes from red hot chilli peppers. These powerful little pods originated in South America, but now form a very important part of many of the world's major cuisines.

India is the largest producer and exporter of chillies, with much of the crop used for local consumption. Thailand, Mexico, Japan, Turkey, Nigeria, Ethiopia, Uganda, Kenya and Tanzania are also prime producers, exporting chillies to other countries around the globe.

The word chilli is spelt in different ways. Sometimes it is chile, sometimes chili, sometimes chilli pepper. This last description is accurate insofar as it recognizes that chillies are members of the *Capsicum* genus, like the sweet peppers. It also forms a link with all those spicy powders – chilli, cayenne and paprika – which are an essential part of many national dishes.

WHAT'S IN A NAME?

The great explorer Columbus was responsible for confusing chillies with peppers. When he set sail in 1492, hoping to find a sea route to the spice islands, it was a source of black pepper (*Piper nigrum*) he was seeking.

Not only did he fail to find his intended destination, discovering instead the Caribbean island of San Salvador (now Watling Island), but he also made the incorrect assumption that the hot spice flavouring the local food was black pepper. By the time it was realized that the fleshy pods of a fruit were responsible, rather than tiny black peppercorns, it was too late.

Below: Mexican chillies, clockwise from top left: small green chillies, chipotle chillies, mulato chillies, dried habanero chillies, pasilla chillies, green (bell) peppers, green jalapeño chillies, Anaheim chillies, and (centre left) Scotch bonnets, (centre right) red chillies.

Above: Chillies form an important part of many of the world's major cuisines.

The Spanish called the flavouring pimiento (pepper) and the name stuck, and it has led to confusion ever since.

It was the Aztecs who coined the name chilli. Like the Mayas and Incas, they were greatly enamoured of the brightly coloured fruit that had originated in the rainforests of South America, and used chillies both as food and for medicinal purposes. When the Spanish invaded Mexico in 1509, they found many different varieties of both fresh and dried chilli on sale at the market at Tenochtitlan and still more being cultivated in Montezuma's botanical gardens at Huaxtepec.

Mexico remains a mecca for chilli-lovers, with every region having its own special varieties. Chillies are valued for their heat and for their flavour, and accomplished Mexican cooks will often use several different types – fresh and dried – in a single dish.

A CHAIN OF CHILLIES

Columbus is credited with introducing chillies to Europe, bringing back "peppers of many kinds and colours" when he returned to Europe in 1493. Soon after this, Vasco da Gama succeeded in finding the sea route to the spice islands. By the middle of the 16th century, a two-way trade had been established. Spices such as nutmeg, cinnamon and black pepper were brought to Europe from the East, and chillies and other plants from the New World went to Asia.

The spice trade created a culinary explosion, and the chilli rapidly became an important ingredient in the food of

Above: Chillies in all their different guises add both flavour and heat to many kinds of dishes. Here, they are shown fresh and dried, preserved in oil and ground into rich and fragrant powders.

Below: Asian chillies

South-east Asia, India and China. Portuguese and Arab traders introduced it to Africa. It was enthusiastically adopted, and when West African slaves were taken to the southern states of America to work the cotton plantations, the chillies that were part of their diet went with them.

THE CHILLI IN EUROPE

Although parts of Europe adopted the chilli with great enthusiasm, universal acceptance has been relatively slow. Spain and Portugal use chillies quite extensively, which is not surprising, given the influence of those early explorers, but in France their use is limited to a few signature dishes, like the fiery rouille traditionally served with bouillabaisse.

It used to be the case that the further north you went, the less likely you would be to encounter chilli dishes. All this is changing, however, as Asian food becomes increasingly popular. Don't be

surprised if you encounter chilli ice lollies (popsicles) or chilli ice cream. The flavour of chillies can be subtle as well as strident, and their affinity for fruit means that, used judiciously, they can make as valuable a contribution to fruit salads as they do to salsas and spicy Mexican dishes.

In response to public demand, most supermarkets stock chillies. Chillies are easy to grow, and many gardeners enjoy cultivating and then cooking them.

Chillies are Good for You
An excellent source of vitamin C, chillies also yield beta carotene, folate, potassium and vitamin E. They stimulate the appetite and improve circulation, but can irritate the stomach if eaten to excess. Chillies are also a powerful decongestant, and can help to clear blocked sinuses.

THE CHILLI FAMILY

There are more than two hundred different types of chilli, all members of the nightshade (Solanaceae) family, like tomatoes and potatoes. Most of those used for culinary purposes belong to the species *Capsicum annuum*. These were originally thought to be annuals, which explains the name, but can be perennial when cultivated in the tropics. The plants grow to a height of 1m/1yd, and chillies of this type include jalapeños, cayennes, Anaheim chillies and poblanos, as well as the common sweet (bell) peppers.

Tabasco chillies and the very hot Punjab chillies belong to a group called *Capsicum frutescens*, while Scotch bonnets and habaneros – the fragrant hot chillies that look like tam-o'-shanters – are *Capsicum chinense*. Some of the largest chilli plants are *Capsicum baccatum*. Ajis fall into this category, as do peri-peri chillies. Finally, there is a small group called *Capsicum pubescens*. The most notable chilli in this group is the manzano. The name means "apple", and these chillies resemble crab apples in size and shape.

Unless you grow chillies or are lucky enough to live near a farmer's market that features these flavoursome ingredients, you are unlikely to encounter more than a few of the more common varieties, such as serranos, jalapeños

Below: Chillies are members of the nightshade (Solanaceae) family, like tomatoes and potatoes.

Above: Capsicum chinense is the species in which fragrant hot chillies such as habaneros are included.

and cayennes, and even these may not be identified as such. Supermarkets have a habit of limiting their labelling to the obvious, like "red chillies" or – one step better – "hot red chillies".

This raises another issue. How do you know whether a chilli is hot or not? Are small chillies hotter than big ones? Or red chillies hotter than green? The answer to the last two questions is no. Although some of the world's hottest chillies are tiny, there are some large varieties that are real scorchers. Colour isn't an infallible indicator either. Most chillies start out green and ripen to red, but some start yellow and become red, and yet others start yellow and stay yellow, and across the spectrum you'll find hot varieties. To confuse the issue still further, chillies on the same plant can have different degrees of heat, and in at least one type of chilli, the top of the fruit is hotter than the bottom. Fortunately for those of us who like to have some warning as to whether the contents of our shopping basket will be fragrant or fiery, there are rating systems for the heat in chillies. The best known of these grades chillies in Scoville units. Until relatively recently, the world's hottest chilli was reckoned to be the Mexican red savina habanero, which scores 557,000 on the Scoville

scale, but a new contender, the tezpur chilli, has been discovered in India. The tezpur registers a blistering 855,000 Scoville units, and is so hot that it is said to have triggered heart attacks in the unwary or novice taster. Scoville units are useful when it comes to fine comparisons such as these, but working with units measured in this way can be unwieldy. For general classification, a simpler system, which rates chillies out of ten, is more often used.

What makes one chilli hotter than another is the amount of the chemical capsaicin contained in the seeds and fibrous white lining. Apart from producing anything from a tingle to a tidal wave of heat, capsaicin also contributes to the feel-good factor by stimulating the brain to produce hormones called endorphins.

A less appealing aspect to capsaicin is that it is an irritant, and can cause severe burning to delicate parts of the face (and other parts of the anatomy) with which it comes into contact. It is therefore vital to handle chillies with care. Wear gloves while preparing them, or cut them up using a knife and fork. If you do handle chillies directly, wash your hands thoroughly in soapy water immediately afterwards (capsaicin does not dissolve in water alone) or use vegetable oil to remove any residue.

THE BURNING QUESTION

If you bite into a chilli that is unpleasantly hot, don't drink a glass of water. That will only spread the discomfort around your mouth making the burning sensation much worse. Instead, try one of these simple solutions:
• Take a large drink of creamy milk, hold it in your mouth for a minute or so, then spit it out discreetly. Repeat as necessary.
• A similar effect can be achieved with water or ice cream, as long as you do not swallow it.
• Eat a piece of fresh bread, a cooked potato or some rice. These will absorb the offending capsaicin oil.

NAMING THE CHILLI

You will find both fresh and dried chillies on sale. Dried chillies can be stored like other spices, and can be rehydrated with excellent results. Some chillies actually taste better when they have been dried. It is well worth getting to know as many different varieties as possible. Then, like a true aficionado, you can start blending several types for the ultimate in chilli pleasure.

The following descriptions of chillies are listed by their heat scale, with 10 being the hottest.

Anaheim

Heat scale 2–3: Their alternative name of "California long green" gives some idea of what these large chillies look like (they are also known as New Mexico). The pods are about 15cm/6in long and about 5cm/2in wide, making them good candidates for stuffing. The flavour is fresh and fruity, like a cross between tart apples and green (bell) peppers. Anaheim skins can be a bit tough, so these chillies are best roasted and peeled. The dried chillies are used to make a mild chilli powder.

Below: Ancho chillies

Ancho

Heat scale 3: Dried poblanos, these are larger than most other dried chillies. Open the packet and savour the wonderful fruity aroma – like dates or dried figs. After rehydration, anchos can be stuffed, and they also taste great sliced or chopped in stir-fries and similar dishes.

Guajillo

Heat scale 3: These dried chillies are about 15cm/6in long, with rough skin. The mature fresh pods are a deep reddish brown and have a smooth texture. It is thought they might be related to Anaheim chillies, as they have a similar look. They have a mild, slightly bitter flavour, suggestive of green tea. Guajillos are used in many classic salsas.

Italia

Heat scale 3: Juicy and refreshing, these dark green chillies ripen to a rich, dark red. They taste great in salads and have an affinity for tropical fruit, especially mangoes.

Below: Mulato chillies

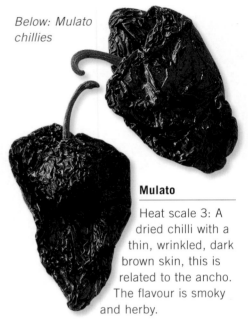

Mulato

Heat scale 3: A dried chilli with a thin, wrinkled, dark brown skin, this is related to the ancho. The flavour is smoky and herby.

Poblano

Heat scale 3: Big and beautiful, poblanos look like sweet (bell) peppers, and are perfect for stuffing. They start off a deep green and ripen to a bright, clear red or rich, dark brown. The flavour is spicier than that of a sweet pepper, with peachy overtones. Poblanos taste wonderful with other chillies, whose flavour they appear to boost.

Below: Poblano chillies

Above: Anaheim chilli

Above: Guajillo chillies

Below: Pasado chillies

Cherry Hot

Heat scale 4: Pungent, with thick walls, these chillies look like large versions of the fruit for which they are named. The skins can be tough, so they are best peeled. Cherry hot chillies have a sweetish flavour and make good pickles.

Below: Cherry hot chillies

Above: Fresno chillies

Fresno

Heat scale 5: Plump and cylindrical, with tapered ends, these fresh chillies are most often sold red, although you will sometimes find green or yellow ones in the shops. They look rather similar to jalapeños, and can be substituted for them if necessary.

Pasado

Heat scale 3–4: Very dark brown, skinny, dried chillies, these are generally about 10cm/4in long. When rehydrated, they taste lemony, with a hint of cucumber and apple. Pasados have an affinity for black beans, and make a fine salsa. Strips taste good on pizzas.

Below: Cascabel chillies

Cascabel

Heat scale 4: The name translates as "little rattle", and refers to the sound the seeds make inside this round dried chilli. The woody, nutty flavour is best appreciated when the skin is removed. Soak them, then either scrape the flesh off the skin or sieve it. Cascabels are great in stews, soups and salsas.

Chilli Boost
For an instant lift, sprinkle some dried crushed chilli on your food.

Costeno Amarillo

Heat scale 4: Not to be confused with the much hotter aji amarillo, this is a pale orange dried chilli, which is ideal for use in yellow salsas and Mexican *mole* sauce. It has a citrus flavour and is often used to give depth to the flavour of soups and stews.

Pasilla

Heat scale 4: Open a packet of these deep purple dried chillies and the first thing you notice is their rich liquorice aroma. Quite large at about 15cm/6in in length, pasillas have a spicy, fruity flavour that is good with shellfish, *moles* and mushrooms. Pureés made from rehydrated pasillas do not need to be sieved, as the skin is thin.

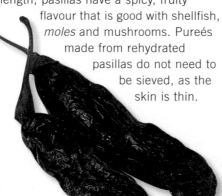

Above: Pasilla chillies

Cultivating Chillies
If you can grow tomatoes, then you'll be able to try your luck with chillies. They enjoy similar conditions, prefer higher temperatures, need watering more often and like slightly acid soils. You can grow them in tubs, hanging baskets or pots on the windowsill. Raise the plants under glass in spring, or buy them from a good plantsman. Plant out when frost is no longer a problem and the first flowers are visible. Water well in dry weather, mulch thickly and feed fortnightly with a high-potash fertilizer. Stake taller varieties. Pinch out growing tips if sideshoots are not being made and stop these once they have set fruit. During the growing season, watch for aphids, cutworms or slugs, and treat. Harvest about 12–16 weeks after planting out. Pull up plants and hang under glass in a sunny place when frost threatens to encourage the fruit to continue ripening.

Hungarian Wax Chillies

Heat scale 5: These really do look waxy, like novelty candles. Unlike many chillies, they start off yellow, not green. It is not necessary to peel them, and they are often used in salads and salsas.

Aji Amarillo

Heat scale 6–7: There are several different varieties of this chilli, including one that is yellow when fully ripe, and a large brown aji that is frequently dried. The chillies average about 10cm/4in in length and look rather like miniature windsocks. Red ajis originated in Peru, and were popular among the Incas.

Above: Chipotle chillies

Above: Jalapeño chillies

Jalapeño

Heat scale 4–7: These are frequently seen in supermarkets. Plump and stubby, like fat fingers, they have shiny skins. They are sold at both the green and the red stage, although the former seem to be marginally more popular. Jalapeños have a piquant, grassy flavour, and are widely used in salsas, salads, dips and stews; they are also canned and bottled. Their fame is due to the fact that they are the best known and most commonly used chilli in Mexican food. A heat-free jalapeño has been developed in the US. Too thick-skinned to be sun-dried, jalapeños are generally smoke-dried and acquire a name change. In this form they are known as chipotle chillies.

Chipotle

Heat scale 6–10: This smoke-dried jalapeño has wrinkled, dark red skin and thick flesh. Chipotles need long, slow cooking to soften them and bring out their full flavour, which is hot and tasty with a deep intriguing smokiness.

Serrano

Heat scale 7: Usually sold green, these are small (about 4cm/1½in long) and quite slender. Serranos are the classic Mexican green chilli (*chiles verdes*), and are an important ingredient in guacamole. The flavour is clean and crisp, with a suggestion of citrus. Serranos are thin-skinned and do not need to be peeled. They dry well, but are seldom sold that way, although you may come across them occasionally for sale in a Mexican or Spanish market.

Below: Cayenne chillies

Below: Pickled jalapeño chillies

Cayenne

Heat scale 6–8: There are several varieties of this very popular chilli, including the familiar "long hot reds". They range from 7.5cm/3in to 17cm/6½ in in length, and have a sweet yet fiery flavour. The basis of cayenne pepper, these chillies are also used in sauces.

Above: Serrano chillies

Left: Bird's eye chillies

Bird's Eye

Heat scale 8: Small and extremely hot, these come from a highly volatile family of chillies that are found in Africa, Asia, the United States and the Caribbean, and often labelled simply as "Thai chillies". Thin-fleshed and explosively hot, they are sold green and red, often with the stems still attached. Dried, they are widely available in jars. They are called bird's eyes because they are much liked by mynah birds.

Below: Dried bird's eye chillies

Tiny Terrors
Thailand grows many different varieties of chillies.The smallest are so tiny they are popularly referred to as *prik kee noo* (mouse droppings). Use cautiously as they are fiery hot.

De Arbol

Heat scale 8: More often sold dried than fresh, these smooth cayenne-type chillies are slim and curvacious. A warm orange-red, they are about 7.5cm/3in long. De arbols combine blistering heat with a clean, grassy flavour. Add them to soups or use to enliven vinegar or oil. Unlike most dried chillies, which must be soaked in hot water for 20–30 minutes before use, dry de arbol pods can be crumbled and added straight to stews or similar dishes. To reduce the heat, slit them and shake out the seeds first.

Above: Dried de arbol chillies

Manzano

Heat scale 9: This delicious chilli is very hot and fruity. About the size of a crab apple, it is the only chilli to have purple/black seeds.

Habanero

Heat scale 10: Don't imagine that intense heat is the only defining feature of this lantern-shaped chilli. Habaneros have a wonderful, fruity flavour, and a surprisingly delicate aroma. Some say it

Above: Dried habanero chillies

reminds them of chardonnay wine; others that it is redolent of sun-warmed apricots. Don't sniff them too enthusiastically, however, and be ultra-cautious when handling habaneros, for they are excessively hot. Always wear strong gloves when preparing them, and don't stand over a food processor or blender when using them to make a paste, or the fumes may burn your face. When cooking with habaneros, a little goes a long way. They are very good with fruit and in salsas. Dried habaneros have medium-thick flesh and wrinkled skins. When rehydrated, they have a rich tropical-fruit flavour.

Scotch Bonnets
Heat scale 10: Often confused with habaneros, which they closely resemble. Scotch bonnets are grown in Jamaican and are the principal ingredient of jerk seasoning.

Below: Scotch bonnet chillies

Use Scotch bonnets very cautiously as they are one of the hottest chillies. It is advisable to deseed them before use unless you can tolerate their intense and lingering flavour.

CHILLI PRODUCTS

Specialist shops, devoted to chillies and chilli products, are springing up all over the world. Alongside mugs, plates, bowls and aprons rioting with chilli motifs, you'll find an astonishing array of powders, pastes, sauces and oils.

POWDERS

Anything connected with chillies tends to be confusing, and chilli powder is no exception. The name suggests that this product is simply powdered chilli, but it is in fact a blend of several ingredients, designed specifically for making chilli con carne. In addition to ground hot chillies, it typically contains cumin, oregano, salt and garlic powder.

Pure powders – the whole chilli and nothing but the chilli – are less easy to come by, but are available from specialist shops and by mail order. Ancho, caribe and Anaheim (New Mexico) red powders are mild (heat scale 3). Pasilla, a rich, dark powder, registers 4 on the heat scale, while chipotle is a little hotter still.

Right: Chilli powder

Left: Ancho powder

Right: Pasilla powder

Left: Paprika

Right: Cayenne pepper

Convenient Chillies

Jars of whole chillies in white wine vinegar are handy for the home cook. Also look out for minced (ground) chillies. After opening, jars must be tightly closed, kept in the refrigerator and the contents consumed by the use-by date.

Cayenne pepper is a very fine ground powder from the *Capsicum frutescens* variety of chilli. The placenta (the fibrous white inner lining) and seeds are included, so it is very hot. Tiny amounts of cayenne are often added to cheese and egg dishes, and it is sprinkled over smoked fish and prawns (shrimp). It is also added to some curries.

Paprika is a fine, rich red powder made from mild chillies. The core and seeds are removed, but the flavour can still be quite pungent. Hungarians have adopted this as their national spice, but it is also widely used in Spanish and Portuguese cooking. Look out for *pimentón dulce*, a delicious smoked paprika from Estramadura in Spain.

Right: Crushed chilli flakes

CRUSHED CHILLIES

Dried chilli flakes are widely available. Italians call them *peperoncini* and add them to their famous arrabiata sauce. Sprinkle them on pizzas or add to cooked dishes for a last-minute lift. Crushed dried green jalapeños are a useful pantry item, combining considerable heat with a delicious, melting sweetness.

CHILLI PASTE

It is worth keeping a few jars of ready-made chilli paste, such as harissa or *ras-el-hanout*, on your shelves. A hot chilli paste is quite easy to make at home. Simply seed fresh chillies, then purée them in a blender or food processor until smooth. Store small amounts in the refrigerator for up to 1 week, or freeze for up to 6 months. Chilli paste can also be made from dried chillies. Having rehydrated them, purée as for fresh chillies. You may have to sieve tough-skinned varieties.

Below: Hot chilli paste

Below: Red Tabasco sauce

Left: Green Tabasco sauce

CHILLI SAUCES

There are many varieties of these and the names appear to prove that chillies stimulate the imagination as well as the appetite. Some of the printable ones include Endorphin Rush, Lethal Weapon and Global Warming, along with the unforgettable Scorned Woman Hot Sauce.

The most famous chilli sauce, however, is Tabasco, developed in Louisiana by E. McIlhenny in the latter half of the 19th century. Chillies are matured in oak barrels to develop the sauce's unique flavour. Try mixing a few drops with fresh lime juice as a baste next time you grill salmon steaks, or add to sauces, soups or casseroles. Also available is Tabasco Jalapeño Sauce – often referred to as green Tabasco sauce. Milder in flavour than the red version, it is good with nachos, hamburgers or on pizza.

Chilli sauces are also widely used in Asia. Chinese chilli sauce is quite hot and spicy, with a hint of fruitiness thanks to the inclusion of apples or plums. For an even milder flavour, look out for sweet chilli sauce, which is a blend of red chillies, sugar and tamarind juice from Sichuan. There is also a thick Chinese sauce made solely from chillies and salt. This is usually sold in jars, and is much hotter than the bottled version. Vietnamese chilli sauce is very hot, while the Thai sauce tends to be thicker and more spicy. Bottled chilli sauces are used both for cooking and as a dip.

CHILLI OILS

Various types of chilli oil are on sale. Toss them with pasta, add a dash to a stir-fry, or drizzle them over pizzas.

Chilli oils also make a good basis for salad dressings. You can make your own chilli oil by heating chillies in oil, or use a ready-made mixture. Olive oil, flavoured with chipotle and de arbol chillies, with a hint of rosemary, is a particularly good blend. It can also be used for light cooking.

Chilli oil is seldom used for cooking in China and South-east Asia, but is a popular dipping sauce. Two types are widely sold. The first is a simple infusion of dried chillies, onions, garlic and salt in vegetable oil. The second, XO chilli oil, is flavoured with dried scallops and costs considerably more. Chilli oil has a pleasant smell, and a concentrated flavour, much stronger than chilli sauce. It is often drizzled over fish and shellfish just before serving. It should be used sparingly.

Below: Chilli oil

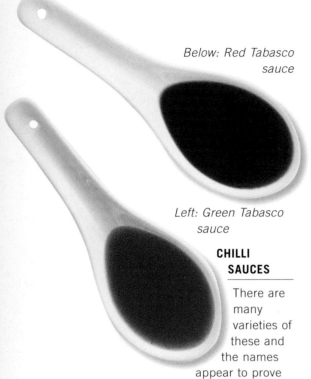

Above: Sweet chilli sauce (top) and chilli sauce

Chilli and Tomato Oil
Heating oil with chillies intensifies the rich flavour. This tastes great sprinkled over pasta.

1 Heat 150ml/¼ pint/⅔ cup olive oil in a pan. When it is very hot, but not smoking, stir in 10ml/2 tsp tomato purée (paste) and 15ml/1 tbsp dried red chilli flakes.

2 Leave to cool, then pour into an airtight jar and store in the refrigerator for up to 2 months.

CHOOSING, STORING AND EQUIPMENT

Below is some helpful advice on selecting and storing chillies and tips on equipment that will make their preparation simpler.

CHOOSING AND STORING CHILLIES

• When buying fresh chillies, apply the same criteria as when buying sweet (bell) peppers. The fruit should look bright and unblemished.
• Some chillies are naturally wrinkled when ripe, however, so a smooth skin is not essential.

Above: Chillies dried on string or canes will keep well for many months.

• Avoid any chillies that seem limp or dry, or that have bruising on the skin.
• In the supermarket, wrap your hand in a plastic bag when picking out chillies, or you may have an unpleasant surprise if you later touch your face.
• To store chillies, wrap them in kitchen paper, place in a plastic bag and keep in the salad compartment of the refrigerator for a week or more.
• Chillies can also be frozen. There is no need to blanch them if you plan to use them fairly soon.
• Frozen chillies are a huge boon to the busy cook, as they can be sliced when only partially thawed, and crushed with garlic and ginger to make a fragrant spice paste.
• To dry chillies, thread them on a string, hang them in a warm place until dry, then crush them and store in a sealed jar.

EQUIPMENT

Gloves may not seem obvious pieces of equipment, but they are invaluable for the dedicated chilli cook. The fine disposable gloves used in hospitals can be used for most chillies, but you need the heavy-duty type for really hot varieties such as habaneros. Of course, you can prepare chillies without wearing gloves, either by using a knife and fork for cutting, or by taking a chance and washing your hands in soapy water afterwards, but burns from capsaicin, the chemical found in the seeds and fibrous white lining, can be very unpleasant.

A mortar and pestle is ideal for grinding chillies and making chilli pastes, but it does involve a fair amount of hard work. Traditional Indian or Asian granite or stone sets are generally fairly large, with deep, pitted or ridged bowls. The rough surface acts like pumice, increasing the grinding effect. Porous volcanic rock is also used for the Mexican mortar – the *molcajete* – which traditionally stands on wide legs, and is very sturdy. The Mexican *tejolote* tends to be shorter

Left: A smooth mortar and pestle for crushing dry ingredients.

Above: A rough mortar and pestle for making wet pastes.

Left: If you like to make your own spice mixtures, then a spice or coffee grinder kept solely for this purpose is very useful.

than the traditional pestle, and fits neatly into the hand. *Molcajetes* must be tempered before being used. To do this, a mixture of dry rice and salt is spooned into the bowl, then ground into the surface to remove any loose sand or grit before being discarded.

A food processor is faster and easier, if less satisfying, than a mortar and pestle, especially for pastes, but must be very carefully cleaned after use. If you intend preparing chillies and spice pastes frequently, it may be worth investing in a mini food processor, and reserving it for spices.

A spice grinder, or coffee grinder kept specifically for spices, is handy when making dry spice mixtures.

Left: A food processor or a blender will process chillies very efficiently, and is especially useful for large quantities.

PREPARATION AND COOKING TECHNIQUES

Every cook handling chillies has had the same experience, that unthinking moment when the hand goes to the face and the burning, tingling sensation of chilli oil is experienced, especially around the sensitive areas of the eyes, nose and mouth. It's not worth it! So be warned, be careful. Wear rubber gloves or wash your hands thoroughly in plenty of hot soapy water when handling chillies. Water alone will not remove the chemical capsaicin, and even after using soap, traces may remain. Baby oil or olive oil can be used to remove it from sensitive areas. This advice applies to dried and fresh chillies as the burning properties are equally strong for both.

Preparing Fresh Chillies

1 If the chilli is to be stuffed, and kept whole, merely slit it without separating the 2 halves. For all other purposes, hold the chilli firmly at the stalk end, and cut it neatly in half lengthwise with a sharp knife.

2 Cut off the stalk from both halves of the chilli, removing a thin slice containing the stalk from the top of the chilli at the same time. This will help to free the white membrane (placenta) and make it easier to scrape out the seeds to be discarded.

3 Carefully scrape out all the seeds and discard them. Remove the core with a small sharp knife.

4 Cut out any white membrane from the centre of each chilli half. Keep the knife blade close to the flesh so that all the membrane is removed. This is usually easy to do. Discard the membrane.

5 Slice each piece of chilli into thin strips. If diced chilli is needed, bunch the strips together and cut across them to produce tiny pieces.

COOK'S TIP
Much of the capsaicin, the fiery oil in chillies, is concentrated in the fibrous white section that contains the seeds. Many recipes suggest removing and discarding this, but true chilli lovers usually leave it in.

Soaking Dried Chillies

Most dried chillies must be rehydrated before being used. In some instances, a recipe will recommend toasting as a first step, to intensify the flavour. This can be done by putting the seeded chillies in a roasting pan in the oven for a few minutes, or by pressing them on to the surface of a hot, dry, heavy frying pan. Do not let them burn, or they could become bitter. Once this is done, continue as below.

1 Wipe the chillies to remove any surface dirt. If you like, you can slit them and shake out the seeds before soaking. Alternatively, just brush away any seeds you can see.

2 Put the chillies in a bowl and pour over hot water to cover. If necessary, fit a saucer in the bowl to keep the chillies submerged. Soak for 20–30 minutes (up to 1 hour if possible), until the colour is restored and the chillies have softened and swelled.

3 Drain the chillies, cut off the stalks if necessary, then slit them and scrape out the seeds. Slice or chop the flesh. If the chillies are to be puréed, process them with a little of the soaking water. Sieve the purée if necessary.

Roasting Fresh Chillies

There are several ways of roasting fresh chillies. You use the grill, roast in the oven, dry-fry as explained below, or hold them over a gas flame.

1 Put the chillies in a dry frying pan and place over the heat until the skins are charred and blistered. Alternatively, roast the chillies in a griddle pan.

2 For larger chillies that are to be stuffed, make a neat slit down the side of each one. Place in a dry frying pan over a moderate heat, turning frequently until the skins blister.

3 To roast chillies on a skewer over a flame, spear them on a long-handled metal skewer and roast them over the flame of a gas burner until the skins blister and darken.

4 Slip the roasted chillies into a strong plastic bag and tie the top to keep the steam in.

5 Set aside for 20 minutes. Take the chillies out of the bag and remove the skins, either by peeling them off, or by rubbing the chillies with a clean dishtowel. Cut off the stalks, then slit the chillies and, using a sharp knife, scrape out and discard the seeds.

Grinding Chillies

When making chilli powder, this method gives a distinctive and smoky taste.

1 Soak the chillies, if dried, pat dry and then dry fry in a heavy pan until crisp. You can also do this on a griddle. In either case, watch the chillies carefully because they can suddenly burn, and then you have to start all over again!

2 Transfer to a mortar and grind to a fine powder with a pestle. Store in an airtight container.

Making a Chilli Flower

This makes a very attractive garnish for a special dish.

1 Wearing rubber gloves and using a small pair of scissors or a slim-bladed knife, cut a chilli carefully lengthwise from the tip to within 1cm/½in of the stem end. Repeat this at regular intervals around the chilli – more cuts will produce more petals.

2 Rinse the chilli in cold water and remove all the seeds. Place in a bowl of iced water and chill for at least 4 hours. For very curly flowers, leave the chilli overnight. When ready to use, lift the chilli out and drain it on kitchen paper.

SPICE POWDERS

The name "curry powder" used to be attached to any ground spice mixture used for making hot or highly flavoured foods. It isn't an authentic term, but is a corruption of the Tamil word "karhi", which simply means a food cooked in a sauce. During the days of the Raj, British merchants and soldiers returning home were eager to continue enjoying the flavours they had encountered in India, and demand for a commercial curry powder was the result. The first of these were crude mixtures, bearing little resemblance to the sophisticated and often subtle blends that Indian cooks produced every day. These differed according to whether they were to be used for meat, poultry, fish or vegetables, and reflected the personal tastes of the maker.

Above: Ancho powder

Today, although bought curry powders have improved greatly, many individuals prefer to make their own spice mixtures in the traditional fashion, roasting and grinding whole spices and savouring the wonderful aroma that is part and parcel of the procedure.

Chillies do not feature in all spice blends, but are typical of those that originated in hot spots such as Madras, Mysore or Goa (the home of vindaloo).

Dry spice mixes – or curry powders – are popular in India, Pakistan and Sri Lanka. Each region has its own favourite blend of spices. When making your own spice powders and pastes, feel free to experiment with different types of dried or fresh chillies. Where chilli powder is listed in recipes, you can opt for the blended spice or a pure powder from a specific type of chilli.

Classic Curry Powder

This mixture can be modified to suit your own personal taste. Try not to keep it too long, or it will lose its aroma.

MAKES ABOUT 115G/4OZ/1 CUP

INGREDIENTS
   6–8 dried red chillies
   105ml/7 tbsp coriander seeds
   60ml/4 tbsp cumin seeds
   10ml/2 tsp fenugreek seeds
   10ml/2 tsp black mustard seeds
   10ml/2 tsp black peppercorns
   15ml/1 tbsp ground turmeric
   5ml/1 tsp ground ginger

1 Unless you like a fiery mixture, snap off the stalks from the dried chillies and shake out and discard most of the seeds and all the stalks.

2 Heat a heavy pan and dry-fry the chillies with the seeds and black peppercorns over a medium heat until they give off a rich aroma. Shake the pan constantly so that the spices are evenly roasted.

3 Tip the roasted spices into a mortar and grind them to a smooth powder. Alternatively, use a spice grinder or a coffee grinder reserved for spices.

4 Stir in the ground turmeric and the ginger. Use immediately or store in an airtight jar protected from strong light.

Below: Classic curry powder

Mild Curry Powder

This is a basic recipe for a mild Indian curry powder, but you can adjust the quantities to suit your taste.

MAKES ABOUT 115G/4OZ/1 CUP

INGREDIENTS
Whole spices
   50g/2oz/½ cup coriander seeds
   60ml/4 tbsp cumin seeds
   30ml/2 tbsp fennel seeds
   30ml/2 tbsp fenugreek seeds
   4 dried red chillies
   5 curry leaves
Ground spices
   15ml/1 tbsp chilli powder
   15ml/1 tbsp ground turmeric
   2.5ml/½ tsp salt

1 Dry-roast the whole spices in a large heavy-based frying pan for 8–10 minutes, shaking the pan from side to side until the spices begin to darken and release a rich aroma. Allow them to cool slightly.

2 Put the spices in a spice grinder or mini food processor and process gently to achieve a fine powder.

3 Add the remaining ground spices and store in an airtight jar.

Garam Masala

Garam means "hot" and masala means "spices" so the spices used are those that "heat" the body, such as chillies, black peppercorns, cinnamon and cloves. Garam masala is added at the end of cooking and sprinkled over dishes as a garnish.

Below: Garam masala

MAKES ABOUT 50G/2OZ/½ CUP

INGREDIENTS
    10 dried red chillies
    2 × 2.5cm/1in cinnamon sticks
    2 curry leaves
    30ml/2 tbsp coriander seeds
    30ml/2 tbsp cumin seeds
    5ml/1 tsp black peppercorns
    5ml/1 tsp cloves
    5ml/1 tsp fenugreek seeds
    5ml/1 tsp black mustard seeds
    1.5ml/¼ tsp chilli powder

1 Dry-fry the chillies, cinnamon sticks and curry leaves in a large heavy frying pan for 2 minutes until you smell the spices as they roast.

2 Add the coriander and cumin seeds, peppercorns, cloves, fenugreek and mustard seeds, and dry-fry for a further 8–10 minutes, shaking the pan from side to side until the spices begin to darken and release a rich aroma.

3 Allow the mixture to cool slightly before grinding. Put the mixture into a spice grinder or electric coffee grinder, kept for spice grinding, or use a pestle and mortar. Grind to a fine powder. Add the chilli powder, mix together and store the powder in an airtight jar.

COOK'S TIP
Garam masala will keep for 2–4 months in an airtight container and the flavours will mature during storage.

> **Keep a lid on it**
> If your pan is a fairly shallow one, put a lid over it when frying the mustard seeds. When they pop, they can travel a surprising distance. Shiver the pan from side to side while the seeds are frying, so that they do not stick to the base. Fry over a gentle heat. You can use this technique for other small seeds, such as cumin.

Sambaar Powder

This blend of spices and dhal is used in South Indian cooking to flavour vegetable and lentil combinations, braised dishes and spicy broths. The powder also acts as a thickening agent.

MAKES ABOUT 105ML/7 TBSP

INGREDIENTS
    8–10 dried red chillies
    90ml/6 tbsp coriander seeds
    30ml/2 tbsp cumin seeds
    10ml/2 tsp black peppercorns
    10ml/2 tsp fenugreek seeds
    10ml/2 tsp urad dhal (white split
        gram beans)
    10ml/2 tsp channa dhal (yellow
        split peas)
    10ml/2 tsp mung dhal (yellow
        mung beans)
    25ml/1½ tbsp ground turmeric

1 Snap off the stalks from the dried chillies and shake out most of the seeds. Heat a heavy frying pan and add the first 5 ingredients.

2 Toss all the spices together over a medium heat until they give off a rich aroma, then turn into a bowl. Repeat the process with the pulses, to toast them without letting them burn.

3 Mix the spices and pulses together, then grind them to a fine powder. Stir in the turmeric. Use immediately or store in an airtight jar away from strong light.

Below: Sambaar powder

Sri Lankan Curry Powder

This has totally different characteristics from Indian curry powders. The spices are roasted separately, and chilli powder is used instead of whole dried chillies. The result is a rich, dark curry powder that is ideal for fish, poultry, meat and vegetable curries.

In Sri Lanka, coriander, cumin, fennel and fenugreek seeds are roasted separately before being combined with roasted cinnamon, cloves and cardamom seeds. After grinding, chilli powder is stirred into the mixture, which is aromatic, rather than fiery. Colour and presentation are key features of Sri Lankan cuisine, and you will often find red, yellow and even black curries artistically arranged around a central bowl of rice.

MAKES ABOUT 75G/3OZ/¾ CUP

INGREDIENTS
    90ml/6 tbsp coriander seeds
    45ml/3 tbsp cumin seeds
    15ml/1 tbsp fennel seeds
    5ml/1 tsp fenugreek seeds
    5cm/2in piece cinnamon stick
    5ml/1 tsp cloves
    8 green cardamom pods
    6 dried curry leaves
    5–10ml/1–2 tsp chilli powder

1 Dry-fry or roast the coriander seeds, cumin seeds, fennel seeds and fenugreek seeds separately, because they all turn dark at different stages. Do not let the spices burn; remove them as soon as they give off a rich aroma.

2 Dry-fry the cinnamon stick, cloves and cardamom pods together for a few minutes until they give off a pungent aroma.

Above: Sri Lankan curry powder

3 As soon as they are cool enough to handle, remove the seeds from the cardamom pods and place them in a mortar. Add the remaining dry-fried ingredients, then the curry leaves. Grind to a smooth powder. Alternatively, use a spice grinder.

4 Stir in the chilli powder. Use immediately or store in an airtight jar away from strong light.

Singapore-style Curry Powder

Chillies are a key ingredient in this curry powder for poultry and meat dishes.

MAKES ABOUT 75G/3OZ/¾ CUP

INGREDIENTS
    3–4 dried red chillies
    90ml/6 tbsp coriander seeds
    15ml/1 tbsp cumin seeds
    15ml/1 tbsp fennel seeds
    10ml/2 tsp black peppercorns
    2.5cm/1in piece cinnamon stick
    4 green cardamom pods
    6 cloves
    10ml/2 tsp ground turmeric

1 Unless you like a fiery mixture, snap off the stalks from the dried chillies and shake out most of the seeds.

2 Heat a heavy pan and add all the seeds, with the chillies, peppercorns, cinnamon stick, cardamoms and cloves. Dry-fry over a medium heat, stirring, until the spices give off a rich aroma.

Above: Singapore-style curry powder

3 When cool enough to handle, break the cinnamon stick into small pieces and remove the seeds from the cardamom pods.

4 Grind all the roasted spices to a fine powder in a mortar. Alternatively, use a spice grinder or an electric coffee grinder reserved for spices.

5 Stir in the ground turmeric. Use immediately or store in an airtight jar away from strong light.

> **VARIATION**
> To adapt Singapore-style curry powder for using with fish and shellfish, use only 2–3 chillies and 5ml/1 tsp black peppercorns, but increase the fennel seeds to 30ml/ 2 tbsp. Add 5ml/1 tsp fenugreek seeds. Leave out the cinnamon stick, cardamom pods and cloves.
>
>

Seven-seas Curry Powder

Like Sri Lankan Curry Powder, this uses chilli powder rather than whole dried chillies. Milder than some of the other mixtures, it combines the fiery taste of chilli with the warm flavours of cumin, cinnamon and cloves. It is widely used in Indonesian and Malaysian cooking.

MAKES ABOUT 90G/3½OZ/SCANT 1 CUP

INGREDIENTS
  6–8 white cardamom
    pods, bruised
  90ml/6 tbsp coriander seeds
  45ml/3 tbsp cumin seeds
  25ml/1½ tbsp celery seeds
  5cm/2in piece cinnamon stick
    or cassia
  6–8 cloves
  15ml/1 tbsp chilli powder

1 Put the cardamom pods in a heavy frying pan with all the other whole spices. Dry-fry the mixture, stirring it and shaking the pan constantly, until the spices give off a rich, heavy aroma.

2 When they are cool enough to handle, remove the cardamom seeds from the pods, then grind them finely with all the other roasted ingredients.

3 Add the chilli powder and mix. Use immediately or store in an airtight jar.

Below: Seven-seas curry powder

Malayan-Chinese Curry Powder

This is good for poultry, especially chicken, and robust fish curries. You can double or even treble the quantities, but it is better to make a smaller amount and use it fairly quickly, as curry powder will stale if stored for too long.

MAKES ABOUT 60ML/4 TBSP

INGREDIENTS
  2 dried red chillies
  6 whole cloves
  1 small cinnamon stick
  5ml/1 tsp coriander seeds
  5ml/1 tsp fennel seeds
  10ml/2 tsp Sichuan peppercorns
  2.5ml/½ tsp grated nutmeg
  2.5ml/½ tsp ground star anise
  5ml/1 tsp ground turmeric

1 Snap or cut the tops off the dried chillies and shake out most of the seeds. Use a small, sharp knife to remove any remaining seeds.

2 Put the chillies, cloves, cinnamon stick, coriander seeds and fennel seeds in a wok or heavy frying pan. Add the Sichuan peppercorns. Dry-fry over a medium heat, tossing the spices frequently, until they give off a rich, spicy aroma.

3 Tip the spices into a mortar and grind them to a smooth powder. Alternatively, use a spice grinder or an electric coffee grinder reserved for spices.

4 Stir in the grated nutmeg, star anise and turmeric. Use immediately or store in an airtight jar away from strong light to keep its flavour.

COOK'S TIPS
• When you are buying spices, always go to stores where there will be a good turnover. Indian or Asian speciality stores would be ideal. Whole spices do not have an indefinite shelf life, and you want to get the best flavour from your spice mix. Buy individual spices in small quantities and write the date of purchase on the packet if you are buying them loose and they do not have a "best before" date stamped on them. Then you can check them regularly and throw out any that have been stored for more than a couple of months.
• Although it is best to make curry powder and similar spice mixes in small quantities, a trip to a market with a fine selection of fresh spices might tempt you to make a large amount. Put some of the surplus in small jars as gifts for friends who like to cook, and store the rest in airtight tubs in the freezer.

SPICE PASTES

Unlike powdered blends, pastes are made from what are called "wet spices": lemon grass, fresh ginger, garlic, galangal, shallots, tamarind and chillies. These are traditionally ground using a mortar and pestle, but today a food processor is often used for convenience and speed. Supermarkets stock some excellent ready-made spice pastes, but making your own is simple and highly satisfying. Any surplus paste can be stored in a tub in the freezer.

Thai cooking is based on curry pastes. Thai cooks strive to create a balance between spicy hot, sweet, sour and salty tastes, and their curries reflect this. There are three principal types of curry paste – red, green and sour. Fresh ingredients such as chillies, lemon grass and shallots are given a salty tang with shrimp paste, while citrus juice and rind adds a touch of sourness. Fresh pastes can be bought from any Thai market, but most cooks prefer to make their own as needed. You will find commercial curry powder in Thailand – used in dishes such as stir-fried crab in curry sauce – but pastes are preferred.

Madrasi Masala

Masalas can be dry mixes or pastes. This one belongs to the latter category, and is a blend of dry and wet spices. The paste is cooked in oil to develop the flavours.

MAKES ABOUT 450G/1LB/2½ CUPS

INGREDIENTS
    120ml/8 tbsp coriander seeds
    60ml/4 tbsp cumin seeds
    15ml/1 tbsp black peppercorns
    15ml/1 tbsp black mustard seeds
    165ml/11 tbsp ground turmeric
    45–60ml/3–4 tbsp chilli powder
    15ml/1 tbsp salt
    8 garlic cloves, crushed
    7.5cm/3in piece fresh root ginger,
       peeled and finely grated
    about 60ml/4 tbsp cider vinegar
    175ml/6fl oz/¾ cup sunflower oil

1 Heat a heavy frying pan and dry-fry the coriander seeds, cumin seeds and peppercorns for 1–2 minutes, stirring.

Above: Madrasi masala

2 Add the mustard seeds and toss constantly over the heat until they start to pop and the mixture gives off a rich aroma. Do not let the spices become too dark.

3 Grind the mixture to a fine powder, then add the turmeric, chilli and salt. Stir in the garlic, ginger and enough of the vinegar to make a paste.

4 Heat the oil in a large frying pan and fry the paste, stirring and turning it constantly, until the oil begins to separate from the spicy mixture.

5 Spoon the masala into a clean jar. Make sure that there is a film of oil floating on top. This will form an airtight seal and act as a preservative, ensuring that the paste keeps its colour. Store in the refrigerator for 2–3 weeks.

Thai Red Curry Paste

Some excellent versions of this classic paste are now produced commercially, but if you prefer to make your own, here's how.

MAKES ABOUT 175G/6OZ/1 CUP

INGREDIENTS
    3 lemon grass stalks
    10 fresh red chillies, seeded
       and sliced
    115g/4oz dark red onions or
       shallots, chopped
    4 garlic cloves
    1cm/½in piece fresh galangal,
       peeled, sliced and bruised
    stems from 4 fresh coriander
       (cilantro) sprigs
    15–30ml/1–2 tbsp groundnut
       (peanut) oil
    5ml/1 tsp grated dried
       citrus rind
    1cm/½in cube of shrimp paste,
       wrapped in foil and warmed in a
       frying pan
    15ml/1 tbsp coriander seeds
    10ml/2 tsp cumin seeds
    5ml/1 tsp salt

1 Slice the tender lower portion of the lemon grass stalks and bruise them with a cleaver. Put them in a large mortar and add the chillies, onions or shallots, garlic, galangal and coriander stems.

2 Grind with a pestle, gradually adding the oil until the mixture forms a paste. Alternatively, purée the ingredients in a food processor or blender. Add the citrus rind and the shrimp paste. Mix well.

3 Dry-fry the coriander seeds and cumin seeds in a frying pan, then tip them into a large mortar and grind to a powder. Stir into the spice paste, with the salt.

4 Use the paste immediately, or scrape it into a glass jar. Cover with clear film (plastic wrap) and an airtight lid, then store in the refrigerator for 3–4 weeks.

Left: Thai red curry paste

Green Curry Paste

This medium-hot curry paste with its vivid green colour is based on chillies. It is good used with lamb, beef or chicken.

MAKES ABOUT 75G/3OZ/½ CUP

INGREDIENTS
2 lemon grass stalks
15 fresh hot green chillies
3 shallots, sliced
2 garlic cloves
15ml/1 tbsp chopped fresh galangal
4 kaffir lime leaves, chopped
2.5ml/½ tsp grated kaffir
    lime rind
5ml/1 tsp chopped coriander
    (cilantro) root
6 black peppercorns
5ml/1 tsp coriander seeds, roasted
5ml/1 tsp cumin seeds, roasted
15ml/1 tbsp granulated sugar
5ml/1 tsp salt
15–30ml/1–2 tbsp groundnut
    (peanut) oil

1 Slice the tender lower portion of the lemon grass and bruise with a cleaver. Put them in a large mortar and add all the remaining ingredients except the oil. Grind to a paste. Add the oil, a little at a time, blending between each addition.

2 Use the paste immediately, or scrape it into a glass jar. Cover with clear film (plastic wrap) and an airtight lid. Store in the refrigerator for 3–4 weeks.

Below: Green curry paste

Thai Mussaman Curry Paste

Originating from the Malaysian border area, this paste can be used with beef, chicken or duck.

MAKES ABOUT 175G/6OZ/1 CUP

INGREDIENTS
12 large dried red chillies
1 lemon grass stalk
60ml/4 tbsp chopped shallots
5 garlic cloves, roughly chopped
10ml/2 tsp chopped fresh galangal
    or fresh root ginger
5ml/1 tsp cumin seeds
15ml/1 tbsp coriander seeds
2 cloves
6 black peppercorns
1cm/½ in cube of shrimp paste,
    wrapped in foil and warmed in a
    frying pan
5ml/1 tsp salt
5ml/1 tsp granulated sugar
30ml/2 tbsp oil

1 Snap the dried chillies and shake out most of the seeds. Discard the stems. Soak the chillies in a bowl of hot water for 20–30 minutes.

2 Cut the tender lower portion of the lemon grass stalk into small pieces, using a small sharp knife. Place in a dry wok. Add the chopped shallots, roughly chopped garlic and galangal or ginger and dry-fry for a moment or two until the mixture gives off an aroma.

3 Stir in the whole cumin seeds, coriander seeds, cloves and peppercorns, and continue to dry-fry over a low heat for 5–6 minutes, stirring constantly. Spoon the mixture into a large mortar.

Above: Thai Mussaman curry paste

4 Drain the soaked chillies and add them to the mortar. Use a pestle to grind the mixture finely, then add the prepared shrimp paste with the salt, granulated sugar and oil. Pound using the pestle until the mixture forms a rough paste. Use as required, then spoon any leftover paste into a jar, seal tightly and store in the refrigerator for up to 4 months.

COOK'S TIP
Shrimp paste is made from fermented shrimps. Also known as blachan, terasi, kapi or ngapi, it is widely used in the cooking of South-east Asia. It is available from Asian food stores and comes in block form, or packed in tiny tubs or jars. It smells rather vile because it is fermented, but the odour vanishes as soon as the paste is cooked. Warming it tempers the raw taste; the easiest way to do this is to wrap a small cube in foil and dry-fry it in a frying pan for about 5 minutes, turning it occasionally to heat evenly.

SAMBALS

When Westerners speak of sambals, they are usually referring to the side dishes served with curry – diced cucumber, sliced bananas and yogurt. These dishes are designed to cool the palate, but true sambals are something else entirely. They are extremely hot sauces or relishes based on chillies. Traditionally, they are served in small bowls, and used like mustard, to pep up other dishes. A sambal can also be a dish cooked with a hot chilli paste.

Chilli Sambal

This Indonesian speciality – *sambal oelek* – is a very simple mixture, made by pounding hot chillies with salt. Tamarind water is sometimes added, and Asian cooks will occasionally temper its heat by stirring ground roasted peanuts into the mixture.

MAKES 450G/1LB/2½ CUPS

INGREDIENTS
   450g/1lb fresh red chillies, seeded
   10ml/2 tsp salt

1 Cut the chillies in half and remove the stems. Using a sharp knife, scrape out and discard the seeds. Bring a pan of water to the boil, add the chillies and cook for 5–8 minutes.

2 Drain the chillies and tip them into a food processor or blender. Process to a rough paste.

3 Add the salt, process briefly to mix, then scrape the paste into a glass jar. Cover with clear film (plastic wrap) and a lid and store in the refrigerator. To serve, spoon into small dishes and offer the sambal as an accompaniment, or use it as suggested in recipes.

Sambal Blachan

Hot chillies can hold their own against strong flavours, as this sambal proves. The shrimp paste gives it a pungent quality, while the lemon or lime juice adds a welcome sharpness. Sambal blachan is frequently served with rice dishes. The rice tempers the heat.

MAKES ABOUT 30ML/2 TBSP

INGREDIENTS
   2–4 fresh red chillies, seeded
   salt
   1cm/½in cube of shrimp paste
   juice of ½ lemon or lime

1 Chop the chillies roughly and place them in a mortar. Add a little salt, then use a pestle to pound them to a paste.

2 Warm the shrimp paste, either by moulding it on to the end of a metal skewer and heating it in a gas flame until the outside begins to look dry, or by wrapping the paste in foil and heating it in a dry frying pan for about 5 minutes.

3 Add the shrimp paste to the chillies and pound to mix well. Stir in lemon or lime juice to taste.

Above: Sambal kecap

Sambal Kecap

Frequently served as a dip with chicken or beef satays, instead of the more usual peanut sauce, this is also delicious with deep-fried chicken.

MAKES ABOUT 150ML/¼ PINT/⅔ CUP

INGREDIENTS
   1 fresh red chilli, seeded and
   finely chopped
   2 garlic cloves, crushed
   60ml/4 tbsp dark soy sauce
   20ml/4 tsp lemon juice or 15ml/
   1 tbsp tamarind juice
   30ml/2 tbsp hot water
   30ml/2 tbsp deep-fried onion
   slices (optional)

1 Place the chopped chilli, crushed garlic and soy sauce in a small bowl. Stir in the lemon or tamarind juice, mix well, then thin with the hot water.

2 Stir in the deep-fried onion slices, if using. Cover and leave the sambal to stand for about 30 minutes before using.

COOK'S TIP
Deep-fried onion slices are very easy to make. Cut 2–3 onions in half, then into very thin slices. Blot these dry on kitchen paper, then add them to hot oil. Lower the heat slightly and cook until the onions have firmed up and browned. Lift out with a slotted spoon, drain on kitchen paper and leave until cold.

Above: Chilli sambal and sambal blachan (right)

Nam Prik Sauce

This is the universal Thai sauce, served solo, with rice or as a dip for fresh vegetables. The quantities can be varied.

MAKES ABOUT 275G/10OZ/1½–2 CUPS

INGREDIENTS
    50g/2oz dried prawns (shrimp)
    1cm/½in cube of shrimp paste, wrapped in foil and warmed in a frying pan
    3–4 garlic cloves, crushed
    3–4 fresh red chillies, seeded and sliced
    50g/2oz peeled cooked prawns (shrimp)
    a few coriander (cilantro) sprigs
    8–10 tiny baby aubergines (eggplant)
    45–60ml/3–4 tbsp lemon or lime juice
    30ml/2 tbsp Thai fish sauce (*nam pla*) or to taste
    10–15ml/2–3 tsp soft light brown sugar

1 Soak the dried prawns in water for 15 minutes. Drain and put in a mortar with the shrimp paste, garlic and chillies. Pound to a paste with a pestle, or process in a food processor. Add the cooked prawns and coriander. Pound or process again until combined.

2 Chop the aubergines roughly and gradually pound them into the sauce. Add the lemon or lime juice, fish sauce and sugar to taste.

Below: Nam prik sauce

Above: Sambal Salamat

Sambal Salamat

This hot tomato sambal is very popular in Indonesia. It has a very strong flavour and should be used sparingly.

MAKES ABOUT 120ML/4FL OZ/½ CUP

INGREDIENTS
    3 ripe tomatoes
    2.5ml/½ tsp salt
    5ml/1 tsp chilli sauce
    60ml/4 tbsp Thai fish sauce (*nam pla*)
    15ml/1 tbsp chopped fresh coriander (cilantro) leaves

1 Cut a small cross in the base of each tomato. Place them in a heatproof bowl and pour over boiling water to cover. Leave the tomatoes in the water for 30 seconds.

2 Lift out the tomatoes with a slotted spoon and plunge them into a bowl of cold water. The skins will have begun to peel back from the crosses. Remove the skins completely, cut the tomatoes in half and squeeze out the seeds. Chop the flesh finely and put it in a bowl.

3 Add the salt, chilli sauce, fish sauce and coriander. Mix well. Set aside for at least 2 hours before serving, so that the flavours can blend.

VARIATION

Use a fresh red chilli instead of chilli sauce, if you prefer. Slit it, remove the seeds and then chop the flesh finely. To give the sambal a slightly smoky flavour, roast the chilli under the grill (broiler) until the skin blisters and begins to blacken, then remove the skin and seeds before chopping the flesh.

Above: Nuoc Cham

Nuoc Cham

In Vietnam, this fiery sauce is used as a condiment, and serves much the same purpose as salt and pepper does in the West. It tastes good with fried spring rolls. Chillies are widely used in Vietnamese cooking, especially in the centre of the country, where it is believed that eating them frequently keeps mosquitoes away and malaria at bay.

MAKES ABOUT 105ML/7 TBSP

INGREDIENTS
    2 fresh red chillies, seeded
    2 garlic cloves, crushed
    15ml/1 tbsp granulated sugar
    45ml/3 tbsp Thai fish sauce (*nam pla*)
    juice of 1 lime or ½ lemon

1 Chop the chillies roughly, place them in a large mortar and use a pestle to pound them to a paste.

2 Scrape the paste into a bowl and add the garlic, sugar and fish sauce. Stir in lime or lemon juice to taste.

African Spice Mixtures

Chillies are not native to Africa. They were introduced by Portuguese and Arab traders, but Africans really warmed to them, partly for the flavour they brought to a diet that was sometimes rather bland, and partly for the cooling effect they had on the skin by promoting perspiration. Today, Africa is an important chilli producer, with Nigeria, Ethiopia, Uganda, Kenya and Tanzania leading the field.

One of the world's most famous chilli pastes – harissa – comes from North Africa. A spicy blend of red chillies, coriander and cumin, it has a host of uses. Moroccan and Tunisian cooks serve it solo or with puréed tomatoes as a side dish for dipping pieces of barbecue-cooked meat. It is wonderful for adding to soups and stews and also serves as the basis of a sauce for serving over couscous.

Right: Large dried red chillies are used in harissa.

Dried chilli spice mixes are also popular in Africa. They invariably include warm spices such as cardamom, cumin, coriander and ginger, and are used with fish, meat and vegetables. The best-known spice mixes are Berbere, which comes from Ethiopia, and *Ras-el-hanout*, a Moroccan chilli powder that can include upwards of 20 different spices. This also comes as a paste. Tsire powder is a simple peanut and spice mixture used in West Africa for coating kebabs.

Harissa

Serve this hot, spicy condiment as a dipping sauce, or stir it into soups or stews. When added to natural (plain) yogurt, it makes a very good marinade for pork or chicken.

MAKES ABOUT 120ML/4FL OZ/½ CUP

INGREDIENTS
12 dried red chillies
15ml/1 tbsp coriander seeds
10ml/2 tsp cumin seeds
2 garlic cloves
2.5ml/½ tsp salt
60–90ml/4–6 tbsp olive oil

1 Snap the chillies and shake out some, but not all, of the seeds. Discard the stems, then put the chillies in a bowl and pour over warm water to cover. Soak for 20–30 minutes, until softened.

2 Meanwhile, dry-fry the coriander seeds and cumin seeds in a frying pan until they give off a rich aroma. Tip them into a mortar and grind them to a powder with a pestle. Tip them into a bowl and set them aside.

3 Put the garlic in the mortar, sprinkle it with the salt, and pound to a paste. Drain the chillies, add them to the paste and pound until it is smooth.

4 Add the spices, then gradually work in the oil, trickling it in and mixing until the sauce is well blended and has a consistency like that of mayonnaise.

Below: Harissa

Above: Tsire powder

Tsire Powder

This simple spice mixture is used as a coating for kebabs throughout West Africa. Cubes of raw meat are first dipped in oil or beaten egg and then coated in the powder. The cooked kebabs are dusted with a little more tsire powder before being served.

MAKES ABOUT 60ML/4 TBSP

INGREDIENTS
50g/2oz/½ cup salted peanuts
5ml/1 tsp mixed spice or apple pie spice
2.5–5ml/½–1 tsp chilli powder
salt

1 Grind the peanuts to a coarse powder in a mortar, blender or food processor.

2 Add the mixed spice or apple pie spice, chilli powder and a little salt. Mix or process until well blended.

3 Use immediately or transfer to an airtight container, close tightly and store in a cool place for up to 6 weeks.

COOK'S TIP
Mixed spice is a commercial mixture of ready ground spices. It typically contains allspice, cinnamon, cloves, ginger and nutmeg. Similar blends are marketed as apple pie spice or pumpkin pie spice. It is best used within 6 months of purchase to enjoy the best flavour.

Above: Berbere

Berbere

Ethiopia produces some of Africa's most delicious food. Dishes, such as the spicy stews, fuelled by the fire of this hot spice mixture, are served on large discs of bread, called *injera*.

MAKES ABOUT 50G/2OZ/SCANT ½ CUP

INGREDIENTS
    10 dried red chillies
    8 white cardamom pods
    5ml/1 tsp cumin seeds
    5ml/1 tsp coriander seeds
    5ml/1 tsp fenugreek seeds
    8 cloves
    5ml/1 tsp allspice berries
    10ml/2 tsp black peppercorns
    5ml/1 tsp ajowan seeds
    5ml/1 tsp ground ginger
    2.5ml/½ tsp grated nutmeg
    30ml/2 tbsp salt

1 Snap the chillies and shake out some of the seeds. Remove the stalks. Heat a heavy frying pan. Bruise the cardamom pods and add them to the pan with the chilli, cumin, coriander, fenugreek, cloves, allspice berries, peppercorns and ajowan seeds. Roast the spices, shaking the pan over a medium heat, until they give off a rich aroma.

2 Seed the cardamoms, then tip all the roasted spices into a large mortar, spice mill or coffee grinder kept specifically for spices. Grind to a fine powder. Stir in the ginger, nutmeg and salt. Use immediately or transfer to an airtight jar.

Baharat

Variations on this spice are to be found in all the countries that border the eastern Mediterranean, from Egypt and Jordan to the Lebanon and Syria. Its use has also spread south, to the Sudan and Ethiopia. An indication of just how fundamental it is to the cooking of these areas is to be found in its Arabic name, which simply translates as "spice". The recipe here is a basic one, but there are umpteen variations, some including cassia bark.

MAKES ABOUT 115G/4OZ/1 CUP

INGREDIENTS
    1 cinnamon stick
    30ml/2 tbsp coriander seeds
    30ml/2 tbsp cumin seeds
    90ml/6 tbsp cardamom seeds
    30ml/2 tbsp cloves
    30ml/2 tbsp black peppercorns
    60ml/4 tbsp paprika
    5ml/1 tsp ground allspice
    10ml/2 tsp grated nutmeg
    10ml/2 tsp chilli powder

1 Grind the cinnamon stick in a spice mill or a coffee grinder kept especially for spices. Tip the ground cinnamon into a bowl.

2 Heat a frying pan. Add the coriander seeds, cumin seeds, cardamom seeds, cloves and peppercorns. Roast the spices, shaking the pan over a medium heat, until they give off a rich aroma and just begin to change colour.

3 Grind the whole roasted spices, in batches if necessary, until they form a fine powder. This can be done using a mortar and pestle. Alternatively use an electric spice mill or coffee grinder.

4 Add the ground spice mixture to the ground cinnamon and mix well to blend the flavours.

5 Stir in the paprika, ground allspice, grated nutmeg and chilli powder. Use immediately, or transfer the spice mixture to an airtight jar and store out of the light in a cool, dry place to retain its colour and strength.

COOK'S TIPS
• Ajowan seeds resemble cumin seeds in appearance. When crushed, they release a powerful aroma reminiscent of thyme. If you can't locate these seeds, use extra cumin instead, or stir in a little dried thyme just before using the spice.
• If you are unlikely to use the Berbere spice mix quickly, store it in an airtight plastic container in the freezer where it will keep for several months.

Ras-el-hanout
What distinguishes this traditional Moroccan spice mixture is its complexity. It can contain more than 20 different ingredients, including dried rose petals. Every spice merchant seems to have a different blend, and recipes are jealously guarded. Chillies are usually in there somewhere, along with cinnamon, cardamom, coriander seeds, cloves, salt, peppercorns, ginger, nutmeg, turmeric, but it is the secret extras – some of which are rumoured to have aphrodisiac qualities – that really set it apart.

BARBECUE SPICE MIXTURES

Spice rubs and marinades are a boon to the barbecue cook, improving the appearance and flavour of cooked meats, poultry and fish while filling the air with a tantalizing aroma. Many of the mixtures are also delicious on roast chicken; just brush the bird lightly with olive oil before cooking, sprinkle the barbecue spice over it and rub in.

Basic Barbecue Spice Mix

Rub this on chops, steaks or portions of chicken. To make a marinade, add the mixture to a glass of red or white wine. Add a few slices of onion and stir in 60ml/4 tbsp of garlic-flavoured oil (or chilli oil if you are feeling adventurous).

MAKES ABOUT 60ML/4 TBSP

INGREDIENTS
    10ml/2 tsp celery seeds
    5ml/1 tsp paprika
    5ml/1 tsp grated nutmeg
    5ml/1 tsp chilli powder
    5ml/1 tsp garlic powder
    5ml/1 tsp onion salt
    10ml/2 tsp dried marjoram
    5ml/1 tsp salt
    5–10ml/1–2 tsp soft light brown sugar
    5ml/1 tsp lightly ground black pepper

1 Put the celery seeds in a mortar and grind to a powder with a pestle, or use a spice mill. Tip the powder into a bowl and stir in the remaining ingredients. Use the spice mixture immediately or store in an airtight jar.

Below: Basic barbecue spice mix

Above: Old-fashioned Philadelphia spice powder

Old-fashioned Philadelphia Spice Powder

This only has a trace of chilli, but the taste combines well with the warm, rounded flavours of the nutmeg and mace. The mixture makes a truly great seasoning for a pork joint, or can be rubbed both on steaks and chops. Do this in plenty of time before you plan to roast or cook on the barbecue, to allow the flavours to develop.

MAKES ABOUT 30–45ML/2–3 TBSP

INGREDIENTS
    8 cloves
    5ml/1 tsp chilli powder
    2.5ml/½ tsp grated nutmeg
    1.5ml/¼ tsp ground mace
    5ml/1 tsp dried basil
    5ml/1 tsp dried thyme
    2 dried bay leaves
    salt

1 Grind the cloves to a coarse powder, then add the other ingredients and continue grinding until fine.

2 Use immediately or store in an airtight container, away from strong light.

COOK'S TIP
All spices and spice mixtures start to deteriorate soon after being ground, so try to use them as soon as possible. Store in airtight and preferably tinted glass jars in a cool place, away from direct light, or keep them in the freezer.

Jamaican Jerk Paste

Give pork chops or chicken pieces a taste-lift by marinating them in this delectable paste. Scotch bonnet chillies would be used in Jamaica, but they are extremely hot, so unless you are a devout chilli-head, you might prefer to substitute a milder variety, or reduce the quantity.

SUFFICIENT FOR FOUR MEAT PIECES

INGREDIENTS
    15ml/1 tbsp oil
    2 onions, finely chopped
    2 fresh red chillies, seeded and
      finely chopped
    1 garlic clove, crushed
    2.5cm/1in piece of fresh root
      ginger, grated
    5ml/1 tsp dried thyme
    5ml/1 tsp ground allspice
    5ml/1 tsp Tabasco sauce or other
      hot pepper sauce
    30ml/2 tbsp rum
    grated rind and juice of 1 lime
    salt and ground black pepper

1 Heat the oil in a frying pan. Add the onions and cook for 10 minutes until soft. Stir in the chillies, garlic, ginger, thyme and allspice, and fry for 2 minutes more. Stir in the Tabasco sauce or hot pepper sauce, rum, lime rind and juice.

2 Simmer until the mixture forms a dark paste with a rich aroma. Season with salt and pepper, and leave to cool.

3 To use, rub over chops or chicken pieces, place in a shallow dish, cover and chill for 8 hours or overnight before cooking on a barbecue or roasting.

Chermoula

This Moroccan mixture makes a very good marinade for meaty fish, but you can also use it as a cold sauce for fried fish. It is important not to use too much onion.

SUFFICIENT FOR 675G/1½LB FISH FILLETS

INGREDIENTS
1 small red onion, finely chopped
2 garlic cloves, crushed
1 fresh red chilli, seeded and
   finely chopped
30ml/2 tbsp chopped fresh
   coriander (cilantro)
15ml/1 tbsp chopped fresh mint
5ml/1 tsp ground cumin
5ml/1 tsp paprika
generous pinch of saffron threads
60ml/4 tbsp olive oil
juice of 1 lemon
generous pinch of salt

1 Mix the onion, garlic, chilli, coriander, mint, cumin, paprika and saffron threads in a bowl. Add the olive oil, lemon juice and the salt. Mix well.

2 To use, add cubed fish to the bowl and toss until coated. Cover and leave in a cool place to marinate for 1 hour. Thread on to skewers and barbecue or grill (broil).

Thai Chilli and Citrus Marinade

This delectable combination of hot and sour flavours is perfect for chicken and seafood. Marinate fish or shellfish for about 1 hour; chicken for 3–4 hours.

MAKES ABOUT 175ML/6FL OZ/¾ CUP

INGREDIENTS
2 small fresh red chillies
15ml/1 tbsp granulated sugar
2 garlic cloves, crushed
white parts of 3 spring onions
   (scallions), chopped
2.5cm/1in piece of fresh galangal or
   ginger, peeled and finely chopped
grated rind and juice of
   1 mandarin
15ml/1 tbsp tamarind juice
15ml/1 tbsp Thai fish sauce
   (*nam pla*)
30ml/2 tbsp light soy sauce
juice of 1 lime
15ml/1 tbsp vegetable oil

1 Slit the chillies and scrape out the seeds. Chop the flesh roughly and put it in a mortar. Add the sugar and grind to a paste with a pestle.

2 Add the crushed garlic, chopped spring onions and chopped fresh galangal or ginger. Add the grated rind of the mandarin to the mortar. Grind to a paste.

3 Scrape the paste into a bowl. Squeeze the juice from the mandarin and add it to the paste, with the tamarind juice, fish sauce and soy sauce. Stir in the lime juice and oil, mixing well. Set the marinade aside for 30 minutes, to allow the flavours to blend before using as a marinade.

Peri-peri Barbecue Marinade

Peri-peri is a hot chilli sauce that originated in Portugal, but which is now popular wherever there are large Portuguese communities. It is widely used in South Africa and Mozambique, and makes a marvellous marinade that is particularly good with shellfish.

MAKES ABOUT 75ML/5 TBSP

INGREDIENTS
1 fresh red chilli
2.5ml/½ tsp paprika
2.5ml/½ tsp ground coriander
1 garlic clove, crushed
juice of 1 lime
30ml/2 tbsp olive oil
salt and ground black pepper

1 Slit the chilli using a small sharp knife and scrape out and discard the seeds. Chop the flesh finely and put it in a small bowl.

2 Stir in the paprika, ground coriander, crushed garlic and lime juice, then whisk in the olive oil, using a fork or salad dressing whisk. Season to taste with salt and pepper. This makes an excellent marinade for prawns (shrimp) and can also be used with chicken. Marinate prawns for about 30 minutes; chicken for several hours. When cooking the shellfish or chicken on the barbecue, baste it with any of the remaining marinade.

COOK'S TIP
Tamarind pods yield a sour, fruity pulp that is as widely used in South-east Asia as lemon is in the West. Buy tamarind as a compressed block, in slices or as a concentrate. To use block tamarind, pinch off the equivalent of 15ml/1 tbsp and soak this in 150ml/¼ pint/⅔ cup warm water for 10 minutes. Swirl the tamarind with your fingers to release the pulp from the seeds, then strain the liquid through a nylon sieve into a bowl. Tamarind slices must also be soaked in warm water, while the concentrate is mixed with warm water in the ratio of 15ml/1 tbsp concentrate to 75ml/ 5 tbsp water.

CAJUN SPICE MIXTURES AND BASTES

Louisiana is home to some of the world's most exciting food, the marriage of French and Creole cooking with Spanish and African influences. The more sophisticated, cosmopolitan style is called Creole, while Cajun cooking is the food of rustic, country people; the trappers and fishers descended from the French who were exiled from Nova Scotia by the British in 1765. They like their food hot and spicy.

Cajun Spice Mix

This can be used as a seasoning for fish steaks, chicken or meat. It can also be used for gumbo, a thick soup or stew that generally contains okra, and for jambalaya.

MAKES ABOUT 150ML/¼ PINT/⅔ CUP

INGREDIENTS
  1 onion
  2 garlic cloves
  5ml/1 tsp black peppercorns
  5ml/1 tsp cumin seeds
  5ml/1 tsp white mustard seeds
  10ml/2 tsp paprika
  5ml/1 tsp chilli powder or
    cayenne pepper
  5ml/1 tsp dried oregano
  10ml/2 tsp dried thyme
  5ml/1 tsp salt

1 Finely chop the onion. Press the garlic firmly with the flat side of a wide-bladed knife to release the skin, then peel and chop it very finely. Set aside until ready to use.

2 Dry-fry the peppercorns, cumin and mustard seeds over a medium heat, to release their flavours, but do not allow them to burn.

3 Grind the dry-fried spices to a fine powder, then add the paprika, chilli powder or cayenne, oregano, thyme and salt. Grind again to achieve a uniformly fine mixture.

4 If the mix is to be used immediately, add the spices to the finely chopped garlic and onion in a blender or food processor and process until well combined. Alternatively, store the dry mixture in an airtight container, and add the garlic and onion only when ready to use the spice mix.

Below: Cajun spice mix

COOK'S TIP
A simple way to use this spice mix is as a coating for fish steaks, chicken pieces, pork chops or beef steaks that have been dipped in melted butter to help the spices adhere to the flesh. Fry the coated fish or meat in a large frying pan in hot oil or butter in a kitchen that has a good extractor fan, because the cooking process will produce a lot of smoke that can sting the eyes and produce unpleasant smells.

Chilli Pepper Baste

This sauce was developed by the McIlhenny family, producers of Tabasco sauce, and is quite fiery. Cautious cooks should start off by using less Tabasco in the mixture, adding an extra dash or two at the end if necessary rather than making the sauce too hot initially. It is sufficient to baste four pork chops, duck breast portions or lamb steaks.

MAKES ABOUT 115G/4OZ/½ CUP

INGREDIENTS
  115g/4oz/½ cup butter
  juice of 1 lemon
  15ml/1 tbsp Worcestershire sauce
  7.5ml/1½ tsp Tabasco sauce
  1 garlic clove, finely chopped
  salt and ground black pepper

1 Melt the butter in a small non-aluminium pan. Add the lemon juice and bring the mixture to simmering point over a low heat. Do not let the butter burn or it will taste bitter.

2 Add the Worcestershire and Tabasco sauces and the chopped garlic. Continue cooking over a low heat, without letting the garlic brown, for another 5 minutes. Season with salt and pepper. Meanwhile, preheat the grill (broiler) until hot.

3 Use the baste immediately it is ready, otherwise the butter will solidify, preventing application. Using a large pastry brush, spread the baste over the top of the chosen meat or poultry, grill (broil) for about 5 minutes, then turn over and brush the other side with more baste. Grill until the meat or poultry is cooked to your liking.

CHILLI PASTA

Making your own pasta is great fun, and when you add chillies to the dough, it not only looks good, but it tastes excitingly different, too. A flavoured pasta such as this needs to be served with a simple sauce, or stuffed with crab meat for a special treat.

SERVES FOUR TO SIX

INGREDIENTS
  300g/11oz/2¾ cups flour
    (see Cook's Tip)
  3 eggs
  5–10ml/1–2 tsp dried red
    chilli flakes
  5ml/1 tsp salt

1 Mound the flour on a clean work surface and make a large, deep well in the centre with your hands. Keep the sides of the well quite high, so that when the eggs are added they will not run out. Crack the eggs into the well, then add the chilli flakes and salt.

2 With a table knife or fork, mix the eggs, chilli and salt together, then gradually start incorporating the flour from the sides of the well. Try not to break the sides of the well or the runny mixture will escape and quickly spread over the work surface.

3 As soon as the egg mixture is no longer liquid, dip your fingers in the flour and use them to work the ingredients together until they form a rough and sticky dough. Scrape up any dough that sticks to the work surface with a knife, then scrape this off the knife with your fingers. If the dough is too dry, add a few drops of cold water; if it is too moist, sprinkle a little flour over it.

4 Press the dough into a rough ball and knead it as you would bread. Push it away from you with the heel of your hand, then fold the end of the dough back on itself so that it faces towards you and push it out again. Continue folding the dough back a little further each time and pushing it out until you have folded it back all the way towards you.

5 Give the dough a quarter turn anti-clockwise, then continue kneading, folding and turning for 5 minutes if you intend shaping the dough in a pasta machine, or for 10 minutes if you will be rolling it out by hand. Wrap the kneaded dough in clear film (plastic wrap) and leave to rest for 15–20 minutes at room temperature before rolling and shaping for cooking.

Making Pasta in a Food Processor

This is a quick and simple way of making pasta.

1 Sift the flour into the bowl of the food processor and add the salt and chilli flakes.

2 Crack the eggs into the flour and process the mixture until the dough begins to come together. Tip it out and knead until smooth. Wrap in clear film (plastic wrap) and leave for 30 minutes.

Rolling and Shaping Pasta

For rounded spaghetti shapes, you need a machine, but you can easily make flat shapes or filled pasta by hand.

After the dough has rested, sprinkle plenty of flour over your work surface and begin rolling the dough, rotating it in quarter turns. Roll out until you have a sheet 3mm/⅛in thick. Fold into a wide, flat sausage.

For tagliatelle, cut the rolled pasta into 5mm/¼in strips. For ravioli, cut out two equally sized pieces 35 x 23cm/ 14 x 9in. Space the filling evenly across the pasta and moisten with egg to make the seal. Place the second piece on top, pressing down around the filling to push out the air. Divide using a serrated pastry wheel.

COOK'S TIP

The best flour to use is Farina Bianca 00 or Tipo 00, which is available from some larger supermarkets and good Italian delicatessens. Imported from Italy, this is a fine, soft white wheat flour. If you use ordinary plain (all-purpose) flour, you will find the dough quite difficult to knead and roll, especially by hand. If you can't get 00 flour, use a strong white bread flour.

CHILLI GIFTS

Bright and colourful, chillies make beautiful gifts. For a simple "thank you" to a friend who loves cooking spicy foods, simply tie a bunch of chillies together with a raffia bow. When the occasion calls for a more elaborate present, fill a basket with spices, including bunches of small red and green chillies. Chilli oils and vinegars are always welcome, and you can include a pot of chilli mustard as a special treat.

Above: A decorative chilli and cinnamon rope

Chilli Rope

To make a dried chilli rope, thread red chillies on a long piece of fine string and hang in a cool, airy place. They should retain their rich colour and can be used when quite dry. If you are making the rope as a gift, add a little label with the above instructions.

Chilli Spice Basket

The perfect gift for a house-warming! Choose a pretty basket, preferably a coloured one that will set off the contents. Fill with any or all of the following, or make up your own selection of spices.

> 6–7 fresh red chillies, tied
>   with ribbon
> 6–7 fresh green chillies, tied
>   with ribbon
> cinnamon sticks, tied with ribbon
> whole nutmegs
> cardamom pods packed in a muslin
>   or cheesecloth bag
> lemon grass sticks wrapped in kaffir
>   lime leaves and tied with raffia
> dried pomegranates
> vanilla pods (beans) tied with raffia
> dried orange peel
> coriander seeds and cumin seeds
>   packed in muslin or
>   cheesecloth "purses"

Right: Chilli spice basket

Right: Chilli spice oil

Chilli Spice Oil

This looks very pretty on the kitchen shelf and makes a thoughtful gift. The quantities given are just a guide – use your own artistic flair.

MAKES ABOUT 600ML/1 PINT/2½ CUPS

> 600ml/1 pint/2½ cups extra virgin
>   olive oil
> 1 garlic clove, peeled and halved
> 3 dried red chillies
> 5ml/1 tsp coriander seeds
> 3 allspice berries
> 6 black peppercorns
> 4 juniper berries
> 2 bay leaves

1 Pour oil into a sterilized bottle, filling it three-quarters full. Add the garlic, chillies, coriander, allspice, peppercorns, juniper and bay, then top up with more oil to fill the bottle. Seal tightly and label clearly. Leave in a cool, dark place for 2 weeks. If the flavour is not sufficiently pronounced, leave for another week.

COOK'S TIP
Moulds can grow in oil, so long-term storage is not recommended.

Chilli Spirit

For a drink with a real kick, steep chillies in vodka or sherry. Choose a pale spirit to show off the chillies.

MAKES 1 LITRE/1¾ PINTS/4 CUPS

INGREDIENTS
    25–50g/1–2oz small fresh
    red chillies
    1 litre/1¾ pints/4 cups vodka or
    pale dry sherry

1 Wash and dry the chillies thoroughly with kitchen paper, discarding any that are less than perfect, as these will look unsightly in the bottle. Using a fine cocktail stick or toothpick, prick the chillies all over to release their flavours into the alcohol.

2 Sterilize an attractive glass bottle with a wide enough neck to allow the chillies to pass easily. Pack the chillies tightly in the bottle, pushing them down with a metal or wooden skewer.

3 Top up with vodka or sherry to reach almost to the top of the bottle. Cork tightly and leave in a dark, cool place for at least 10 days, or up to 2 months, shaking the bottle occasionally for the chilli flavour to mingle evenly.

Right: Chilli vinegar

Chilli Vinegar

Pep up soups and sauces with this spicy vinegar, or use to deglaze a pan after cooking beef steaks.

MAKES ABOUT 600ML/1 PINT/2½ CUPS

    8 dried red chillies
    600ml/1 pint/2½ cups red wine
    vinegar or sherry vinegar

1 Place the chillies in a sterilized preserving jar or heatproof bottle. Pour the vinegar into a pan and bring to the boil. Carefully pour the vinegar into the jar or bottle. Cool, cover tightly, and leave to steep for 2 weeks, shaking the jar occasionally.

2 Taste for flavour and strain when sufficiently strong, pouring the vinegar into a clean, sterilized bottle, filled right to the top. Cover tightly, label and store.

VARIATION
Chilli Ho Ho Fill a sterilized bottle with small whole chillies. Top up with sherry vinegar, or spirits such as gin or vodka. Cover tightly or seal with a cork, label clearly and leave for 2 weeks, shaking occasionally.

Chilli and Garlic Mustard

A jar of this makes a great gift to add to a basket of mixed chilli goodies.

MAKES ABOUT 300ML/½ PINT/1¼ CUPS

INGREDIENTS
    1 dried red chilli
    40g/1½oz/¼ cup white mustard seeds
    40g/1½oz/¼ cup black mustard seeds
    50g/2oz/¼ cup soft light brown sugar
    5ml/1 tsp salt
    5ml/1 tsp whole peppercorns
    10ml/2 tsp tomato purée (paste)
    1 large garlic clove
    200ml/7fl oz/scant 1 cup distilled
    malt vinegar

1 Snap the top off the chilli and shake out the seeds. Discard the stem. Put the chilli in a food processor or blender with the mustard seeds, sugar, salt, peppercorns, tomato purée and garlic.

2 Whizz until mixed. Add 15ml/1 tbsp vinegar at a time, processing the mixture until it forms a coarse paste.

3 Leave to stand for 10–15 minutes, to thicken slightly. Spoon into a 300ml/ ½ pint/1¼ cup jar or several smaller jars. Cover the surface of the mustard with clear film (plastic wrap) or a waxed paper disc, seal tightly and label.

Below: Chilli and garlic mustard

Turn up the heat with these sizzling sauces, selected to show just how versatile chillies can be in a supporting role. A spoonful of Sweet Potato and Jalapeño Salsa adds sweetness and spice to all sorts of dishes, from grilled fish to chicken or veal. Hot Hot Habanero Salsa stokes the fire, while Guacamole cools and comforts. Some sauces are based on specific chillies, like chipotle and guajillo, while others leave the choice to you. Add spicy relishes and nibbles, and it's easy to see why this chapter is your passport to chilli heaven.

Salsas, Sauces and Nibbles

GUACAMOLE

ONE OF THE BEST-LOVED MEXICAN SALSAS, THIS BLEND OF CREAMY AVOCADO, TOMATOES, CHILLIES, CORIANDER AND LIME NOW APPEARS ON TABLES THE WORLD OVER.

SERVES SIX TO EIGHT

INGREDIENTS
    4 tomatoes
    4 ripe avocados, preferably fuerte
    juice of 1 lime
    ½ small onion
    2 garlic cloves
    small bunch of fresh coriander
      (cilantro), chopped
    3 fresh red fresno chillies
    salt
    tortilla chips, to serve

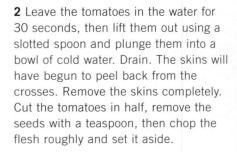

1 Cut a cross in the base of each tomato. Place the tomatoes in a heatproof bowl and pour over boiling water to cover.

2 Leave the tomatoes in the water for 30 seconds, then lift them out using a slotted spoon and plunge them into a bowl of cold water. Drain. The skins will have begun to peel back from the crosses. Remove the skins completely. Cut the tomatoes in half, remove the seeds with a teaspoon, then chop the flesh roughly and set it aside.

3 Cut the avocados in half and remove the stones (pits). Scoop the flesh into a food processor or blender. Process until almost smooth, then scrape into a bowl and stir in the lime juice.

4 Chop the onion finely, then crush the garlic. Add both to the avocado and mix well. Stir in the coriander.

5 Remove the stalks from the chillies, slit them and scrape out and discard the seeds. Chop the chillies finely and add them to the avocado mixture, with the chopped tomatoes. Mix well.

6 Check the seasoning and add salt to taste. Cover closely with clear film (plastic wrap) or a tight-fitting lid and chill for 1 hour before serving as a dip with tortilla chips. If it is well covered, guacamole will keep in the refrigerator for 2–3 days.

COOK'S TIP
Smooth-skinned fuerte avocados are native to Mexico, so would be ideal for this dip. If they are not available, use any avocados, but make sure they are ripe. To test, gently press the top of the avocado; it should give a little.

CLASSIC MEXICAN TOMATO SALSA

THERE ARE VERY MANY RECIPES FOR THIS TRADITIONAL SALSA, BUT ONION, TOMATO, CHILLI AND CORIANDER ARE COMMON TO ALL OF THEM.

SERVES SIX

INGREDIENTS
  3–6 fresh serrano chillies
  1 large white onion
  grated rind and juice of 2 limes,
    plus strips of lime rind,
    to garnish
  8 ripe, firm tomatoes
  large bunch of fresh
    coriander (cilantro)
  1.5ml/¼ tsp sugar
  salt

1 Use 3 chillies for a salsa of medium heat; up to 6 if you like it hot. To peel the chillies, spear them on a long-handled metal skewer and roast them over the flame of a gas burner until the skins blister and darken. Do not let the flesh burn. Alternatively, dry-fry them until the skins are scorched.

2 Place the roasted chillies in a strong plastic bag and tie the top of the bag. Set aside for about 20 minutes.

3 Meanwhile, chop the onion finely, put it in a bowl with the lime rind and juice, and stir the mixture lightly. The lime juice will soften the onion.

4 Remove the chillies from the bag and peel off the skins. Cut off the stalks, slit the chillies and scrape out all the seeds with a knife. Discard the seeds. Chop the flesh and set it aside.

VARIATION
For a smoky flavour, use chipotle chillies instead of fresh serrano chillies.

5 Cut a small cross in the base of each tomato. Place the tomatoes in a heatproof bowl and pour over boiling water to cover.

6 Leave the tomatoes in the water for 30 seconds, then lift them out using a slotted spoon and plunge them into a bowl of cold water to prevent them cooking further. Drain. The skins will have begun to peel back from the crosses. Remove the skins completely.

7 Dice the peeled tomatoes and put them in a bowl. Add the onion and lime mixture. Chop the coriander finely.

8 Add the coriander to the salsa, with the chillies and the sugar. Mix gently until the sugar has dissolved. Season to taste with salt. Cover and chill for 2–3 hours to allow the flavours to blend. The salsa will keep for 3–4 days in the refrigerator. Garnish with the strips of lime rind just before serving.

HOT HOT HABANERO SALSA

THIS IS A VERY FIERY SALSA WITH AN INTENSE HEAT LEVEL. A DAB ON THE PLATE ALONGSIDE A MEAT OR FISH DISH ADDS A FRESH, CLEAN TASTE, BUT THIS IS NOT FOR THE FAINT-HEARTED.

3 Put the chillies in a food processor and add a little of the soaking liquid. Purée to a fine paste. Do not lean over the processor – the fumes may burn your face. Remove the lid and scrape the mixture into a bowl.

4 Put the chopped spring onions in another bowl and add the grapefruit or orange juice, with the lime rind and juice. Roughly chop the coriander.

SERVE SPARINGLY

INGREDIENTS

  5 dried roasted habanero chillies   ·
  4 dried costeno amarillo chillies
  3 spring onions (scallions), chopped
  juice of ½ large grapefruit or
    1 Seville (Temple) orange
  grated rind and juice of 1 lime
  small bunch of fresh
    coriander (cilantro)
  salt

1 Soak the habanero and costeno amarillo chillies in hot water for about 20 minutes until softened. Drain, reserving the soaking water.

2 Wear rubber gloves to handle the habaneros. Remove the stalks from all the chillies, then slit them and scrape out the seeds with a small sharp knife and discard. Chop the flesh roughly.

COOK'S TIP
Dried habanero chillies are just as hot as when fresh. Lantern shaped and deep orange in colour, they release a lovely fruity aroma when reconstituted, and go very well with the milder, citrus-flavoured costeno amarillo chillies.

5 Carefully add the chopped coriander to the chilli mixture and then combine the ingredients very thoroughly. Add salt to taste. Cover the bowl and chill for at least 1 day before use. Serve this salsa very sparingly and warn your guests that it is hot.

SWEET POTATO AND JALAPEÑO SALSA

COLOURFUL AND SWEET, WITH JUST A HINT OF HEAT, THIS SALSA MAKES THE PERFECT ACCOMPANIMENT TO HOT, SPICY MEXICAN DISHES.

SERVES FOUR

INGREDIENTS

675g/1½lb sweet potatoes
juice of 1 small orange
5ml/1 tsp crushed dried
  jalapeño chillies
4 small spring onions (scallions)
juice of 1 small lime (optional)
salt

COOK'S TIP
This fresh and tasty salsa is also very good served with a simple grilled (broiled) salmon fillet or other fish dishes, and makes a delicious accompaniment to veal escalopes (US scallops) or chicken breast portions.

1 Peel the sweet potatoes and dice the flesh finely. Bring a pan of water to the boil. Add the sweet potato and cook for 8–10 minutes, until just soft. Drain off the water, cover the pan and put it back on the stove top, having turned off the heat.

2 Leave for 5 minutes to dry out, tip it into a bowl and set aside.

3 Mix the orange juice and crushed dried chillies in a bowl. Chop the spring onions finely and add them to the juice and chillies.

4 When the sweet potatoes are cool, add the orange juice mixture and toss carefully until all the pieces are coated. Cover the bowl and chill for 2 hours.

5 Taste the salsa and season with salt. Stir in the lime juice if you think the mixture needs to be sharpened slightly. The salsa will keep for 2–3 days in a covered bowl in the refrigerator.

CHIPOTLE SAUCE

THE SMOKY FLAVOUR OF THIS RICH SAUCE MAKES IT IDEAL FOR BARBECUE-COOKED FOOD, EITHER AS A MARINADE OR AS AN ACCOMPANIMENT. IT IS ALSO WONDERFUL STIRRED INTO CREAM CHEESE AS A SANDWICH FILLING WITH CHICKEN. CHIPOTLE CHILLIES ARE SMOKE-DRIED JALAPEÑOS.

SERVES SIX

INGREDIENTS
  500g/1¼lb tomatoes
  5 chipotle chillies
  3 garlic cloves, roughly chopped
  150ml/¼ pint/⅔ cup red wine
  5ml/1 tsp dried oregano
  60ml/4 tbsp clear honey
  5ml/1 tsp American mustard
  2.5ml/½ tsp ground black pepper
  salt

1 Preheat the oven to 200°C/400°F/ Gas 6. Cut the tomatoes into quarters and place them in a roasting pan. Roast for 45–60 minutes, until they are charred.

2 Meanwhile, soak the chillies in a bowl of cold water to cover for about 20 minutes or until soft. Remove the stalks, slit the chillies and scrape out the seeds with a small sharp knife. Discard the seeds. Chop the flesh roughly.

3 Remove the tomatoes from the oven, let them cool slightly, then remove the skins. If you prefer a smooth sauce, remove the seeds. Chop the tomatoes in a blender or food processor. Add the chillies, garlic and red wine. Process until smooth, then add the oregano, honey, mustard and black pepper. Process briefly to mix, then taste and season with salt.

4 Pour the mixture into a small pan. Bring to the boil, lower the heat and simmer the sauce for about 10 minutes, stirring occasionally, until it has reduced and thickened. Spoon into a bowl and serve hot or cold.

GUAJILLO CHILLI SAUCE

THIS SAUCE CAN BE SERVED OVER ENCHILADAS OR STEAMED VEGETABLES. IT IS ALSO GOOD EATEN HOT OR COLD WITH MEATS SUCH AS PORK, AND A LITTLE MAKES A FINE SEASONING FOR SOUPS OR STEWS.

SERVES FOUR

INGREDIENTS
  2 tomatoes
  2 red (bell) peppers, cored, seeded and quartered
  3 garlic cloves, in their skins
  2 ancho chillies
  2 guajillo chillies
  30ml/2 tbsp tomato purée (paste)
  5ml/1 tsp dried oregano
  5ml/1 tsp soft dark brown sugar
  300ml/½ pint/1¼ cups chicken stock

1 Preheat the oven to 200°C/400°F/ Gas 6. Cut the tomatoes into quarters and place them in a roasting pan with the peppers and whole garlic cloves. Roast for 45–60 minutes, until the tomatoes and peppers are slightly charred.

COOK'S TIP
Like chipotle chillies, guajillos are dried. They give the sauce a well-rounded, fruity flavour and do not make it too hot.

2 Put the peppers in a strong plastic bag and tie the top to keep the steam in. Set aside for 20 minutes. Remove the skin from the tomatoes. Soak the chillies in boiling water for 20 minutes.

3 Remove the peppers from the bag and rub off the skins. Cut them in half, remove the cores and seeds, then chop the flesh roughly and put it in a food processor or blender. Drain the chillies, remove the stalks, then slit them and scrape out and discard the seeds. Chop them roughly and add to the peppers.

4 Add the roasted tomatoes to the food processor. Squeeze the roasted garlic out of the skins and add to the tomato mixture, with the tomato purée, oregano, sugar and stock. Process until smooth.

5 Pour the mixture into a pan, place over a medium heat and bring to the boil. Lower the heat and simmer for 10–15 minutes until the sauce has reduced to about half. Transfer to a bowl and serve. Or leave to cool, then chill until required. The sauce will keep in the refrigerator for up to 1 week.

THAI RED CURRY SAUCE

SERVE THIS WITH MINI SPRING ROLLS OR SPICY INDONESIAN CRACKERS, OR TOSS IT INTO FRESHLY COOKED RICE NOODLES FOR A DELICIOUS MAIN-MEAL ACCOMPANIMENT.

SERVES FOUR

INGREDIENTS
    200ml/7fl oz/scant 1 cup
      coconut cream
    10–15ml/2–3 tsp Thai red
      curry paste
    4 spring onions (scallions), plus
      extra, to garnish
    30ml/2 tbsp chopped fresh
      coriander (cilantro)
    1 fresh red chilli, seeded and thinly
      sliced into rings
    5ml/1 tsp soy sauce
    juice of 1 lime
    granulated sugar, to taste
    25g/1oz/¼ cup dry-roasted peanuts
    salt and ground black pepper

1 Pour the coconut cream into a small bowl and stir in the curry paste.

COOK'S TIP
The dip may be prepared in advance up to the end of step 3. Cover and keep in the refrigerator for up to 4 hours.

2 Trim the spring onions and finely slice them on the diagonal. Stir into the coconut cream with the chopped fresh coriander and chilli.

3 Stir in the soy sauce and fresh lime juice, with sugar, salt and pepper to taste. Pour the sauce into a small serving bowl.

4 Finely chop the dry-roasted peanuts and sprinkle them over the sauce. Garnish with spring onions sliced lengthways into thin curls. Serve immediately.

VARIATION
As an alternative to spring onions, try using baby leeks. You may need only one or two and they can be prepared in the same way.

CHILLI <u>AND</u> RED ONION RAITA

RAITA IS A TRADITIONAL INDIAN ACCOMPANIMENT, A COOLING AGENT TO SERVE WITH HOT CURRIES. IT IS ALSO DELICIOUS SERVED WITH POPPADUMS AS A DIP.

SERVES FOUR

INGREDIENTS
5ml/1 tsp cumin seeds
1 large red onion
1 small garlic clove
1 small fresh green chilli, seeded
150ml/¼ pint/⅔ cup natural
   (plain) yogurt
30ml/2 tbsp chopped fresh coriander
   (cilantro), plus extra, to garnish
about 2.5ml/½ tsp granulated sugar
salt

1 Heat a small pan and dry-fry the cumin seeds for 1–2 minutes, until they release their aroma and begin to pop.

2 Let the seeds cool for a few minutes, then tip them into a mortar and crush them with a pestle. Alternatively, flatten them with the heel of a heavy-bladed knife.

COOK'S TIPS
• For an extra tangy raita, stir in 15ml/ 1 tbsp lemon juice.
• For a thicker consistency, drain off any liquid from the yogurt before adding the ingredients.

3 Cut the red onion in half. Cut a few thin slices for the garnish and chop the rest finely. Crush the garlic, then finely chop the chilli. Stir the onion, garlic and chilli into the yogurt with the crushed cumin seeds and coriander.

4 Add sugar and salt to taste. Spoon the raita into a small bowl, cover and chill until ready to serve. Garnish with the reserved onion slices and extra coriander before serving. The dip will keep for 2 days in the refrigerator.

RED ONION, GARLIC AND CHILLI RELISH

THIS POWERFUL RELISH IS FLAVOURED WITH NORTH AFRICAN SPICES AND PUNCHY PRESERVED LEMONS, AVAILABLE FROM DELICATESSENS AND LARGER SUPERMARKETS OR FROM MIDDLE EASTERN FOOD STORES.

2 Add the garlic cloves and coriander seeds. Cover and cook gently for another 5–8 minutes, stirring occasionally to prevent the onions from browning, until the garlic is beginning to soften.

3 Add a pinch of salt, lots of pepper and the sugar, and cook, uncovered, for 5 minutes. Meanwhile, soak the saffron in the warm water for 5 minutes. Then add the saffron mixture (including the saffron threads) to the onions. Add the cinnamon, chillies and bay leaves. Stir in 30ml/2 tbsp of the sherry vinegar and the orange juice.

4 Cook gently, uncovered, until the onions are very soft and most of the liquid has evaporated. Stir in the preserved lemon and cook gently for 5 minutes. Taste and adjust the seasoning, adding sugar and/or vinegar to balance the flavours. You may not need to add more salt, since the lemons are preserved in it.

5 Serve warm or at room temperature, but not hot or chilled. The relish tastes best the day after it is made. Remove the cinnamon stick before serving.

SERVES SIX

INGREDIENTS
   45ml/3 tbsp olive oil
   3 large red onions, sliced
   2 heads of garlic, separated into
     cloves and peeled
   10ml/2 tsp coriander seeds, crushed
     but not finely ground
   10ml/2 tsp light muscovado (brown)
     sugar, plus a little extra
   pinch of saffron threads
   45ml/3 tbsp warm water
   10cm/2in piece of cinnamon stick
   2–3 small whole dried red chillies
   2 fresh bay leaves
   30–45ml/2–3 tbsp sherry vinegar
   juice of ½ small orange
   30ml/2 tbsp chopped
     preserved lemon
   salt and ground black pepper

1 Heat the oil in a heavy pan. Add the onions and stir, then cover and reduce the heat to the lowest setting. Cook for 10–15 minutes, stirring occasionally, until the onions are very soft but not browned.

COOK'S TIPS
• Although you can use any type of dried chilli in this relish, it is worth looking out for the sweet, mild choricero chillies, which impart a lovely, fruity flavour but no heat. Alternatively, use a combination of dried hot and mild chillies.
• If you do not have a pestle and mortar with which to crush the coriander, put the seeds into a small, strong plastic bag and crush under a rolling pin or heavy object.
• Saffron has a strong, slightly bitter flavour, a pungent sweet scent, and is brilliant yellow when soaked.

CHILLI AND ONION RELISH WITH LIME

THIS FRESH RELISH IS IDEAL FOR SERVING WITH STEWS, RICE DISHES OR BEAN DISHES. THE OREGANO ADDS A SWEET NOTE WHILE THE ABSENCE OF SUGAR OR OIL MAKES THIS A VERY HEALTHY CHOICE.

MAKES ABOUT 60ML/4 TBSP

INGREDIENTS
10 fresh green chillies
½ white onion
4 limes
2.5ml/½ tsp dried oregano
salt

COOK'S TIP
This method of roasting chillies is ideal if you need more than one or two, or if you do not have a gas burner. To roast over a burner, spear the chillies, four or five at a time, on a long-handled metal skewer and hold them over the flame, turning them round frequently, until the skins blister.

1 Roast the chillies in a griddle pan over a medium heat until the skins are charred and blistered but not blackened, as this might make the salsa bitter. Place the roasted chillies in a strong plastic bag and tie the top to keep the steam in. Set aside for 20 minutes.

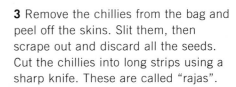

2 Meanwhile, slice the onion very thinly and put it in a large bowl. Squeeze the limes and add the juice to the bowl, with any pulp that gathers in the strainer. The lime juice will have the effect of softening the onion. Stir in the oregano.

3 Remove the chillies from the bag and peel off the skins. Slit them, then scrape out and discard all the seeds. Cut the chillies into long strips using a sharp knife. These are called "rajas".

4 Add the chilli strips to the onion mixture and season lightly with salt. Cover the bowl and chill for at least 1 day before serving, to allow the flavours to blend. Taste the salsa and add more salt at this stage if necessary. The salsa will keep for up to 2 weeks in a covered bowl in the refrigerator.

VARIATION
White onions have a mild sweet flavour, as do red onions, which could equally well be used in their place. The colour combination of red and green would look particularly good with rice dishes.

MIXED SPICED NUTS

SPICE UP YOUR VERY OWN HAPPY HOUR WITH THESE SUPERB SNACKS. THEY ARE EXCELLENT WITH DRINKS.

SERVES FOUR TO SIX

INGREDIENTS
 75g/3oz/1 cup dried unsweetened
   coconut flakes
 75ml/5 tbsp groundnut (peanut) oil
 2.5ml/½ tsp hot chilli powder
 5ml/1 tsp paprika
 5ml/1 tsp tomato purée (paste)
 225g/8oz/2 cups unsalted
   cashew nuts
 225g/8oz/2 cups whole
   blanched almonds
 60ml/4 tbsp granulated sugar
 5ml/1 tsp ground cumin
 2.5ml/½ tsp salt
 ground black pepper
 fresh herbs, to garnish

1 Heat a wok, add the coconut flakes
and dry-fry until golden. Tip out on to a
plate and leave to cool.

COOK'S TIP
The nuts can be stored separately for up
to 1 month in an airtight tub.

2 Heat the wok again and add 45ml/
3 tbsp of the oil. When it is hot, add the
chilli powder, paprika and tomato purée.
Stir well, add the cashew nuts and
gently stir-fry until well coated. Drain,
season with pepper and leave to cool.

3 Wipe out the wok with kitchen paper,
heat it, then add the remaining oil.
When the oil is hot, add the almonds
and sprinkle in the sugar. Stir-fry gently
until the almonds are golden brown and
the sugar has caramelized. Place the
cumin and salt in a bowl. Add the hot
almonds, toss well, then leave to cool.

4 Either mix the cashew nuts, almonds
and coconut flakes together or serve
them in separate bowls. Garnish with
sprigs of fresh herbs such as parsley
and coriander.

RED-HOT ROOTS

*COLOURFUL AND CRISP CHIPS, MADE FROM A SELECTION OF ROOT VEGETABLES, TASTE DELICIOUS
WITH A LIGHT DUSTING OF CHILLI SEASONING. SERVE AS AN ACCOMPANIMENT OR AS A TASTY SNACK.*

SERVES FOUR TO SIX

INGREDIENTS
 1 carrot
 2 parsnips
 2 raw beetroot (beets)
 1 sweet potato
 groundnut (peanut) oil, for
   deep-frying
 1.5ml/¼ tsp hot chilli powder
 5ml/1 tsp sea salt flakes

1 Peel all the vegetables, then slice the
carrot and parsnips into long, thin
ribbons and the beetroot and sweet
potato into thin rounds. Pat dry all the
vegetable ribbons and rounds on
kitchen paper.

2 Half-fill a wok with oil. Heat it to
180°C/350°F or until a cube of day-old
bread, added to the oil, browns in about
45 seconds. Add the vegetable slices in
batches and deep-fry for 2–3 minutes
until golden and crisp. Remove and
drain on kitchen paper.

3 Place the chilli powder and sea salt in
a mortar and grind with a pestle to a
coarse powder. Pile up the vegetable
chips on a serving plate, sprinkle over
the spiced salt and serve immediately.

COOK'S TIP
To save time, you can slice the
vegetables using a mandoline or a food
processor fitted with a thin slicing disc.

CHILLI-SPICED PLANTAIN CHIPS

THIS SNACK HAS A LOVELY SWEET TASTE, WHICH IS BALANCED BY THE HEAT FROM THE CHILLI POWDER AND SAUCE. COOK THE CHIPS JUST BEFORE YOU INTEND TO SERVE THEM.

SERVES FOUR

INGREDIENTS
2 large plantains with very
    dark skins
groundnut (peanut) oil, for
    shallow-frying
2.5ml/½ tsp hot chilli powder
5ml/1 tsp ground cinnamon
hot chilli sauce, to serve

1 Peel the plantains. Cut off and throw away the ends, then slice the fruit diagonally into rounds; do not make them too thin.

2 Pour the oil for frying into a small frying pan, to a depth of about 1cm/½in. Heat the oil until it is very hot, watching it closely all the time. Test by carefully adding a slice of plantain; it should float and the oil should immediately bubble up around it.

3 Fry the plantain slices in small batches or the temperature of the oil will drop. When they are golden brown, remove from the oil with a slotted spoon and drain on kitchen paper.

4 Mix the chilli powder with the cinnamon. Put the plantain chips on a serving plate, sprinkle them with the chilli and cinnamon mixture and serve immediately, with a small bowl of hot chilli sauce for dipping.

COOK'S TIP
Plantains are more starchy than the bananas to which they are related, and must be cooked before being eaten. When ready to eat, the skin is almost black.

POPCORN WITH LIME AND CHILLI

IF THE ONLY POPCORN YOU'VE HAD CAME OUT OF A CARTON AT THE CINEMA, TRY THIS MEXICAN SPECIALITY. THE LIME JUICE AND CHILLI POWDER ARE INSPIRED ADDITIONS, AND THE SNACK IS QUITE A HEALTHY CHOICE TO SERVE WITH DRINKS.

MAKES ONE LARGE BOWL

INGREDIENTS
30ml/2 tbsp vegetable oil
225g/8oz/1¼ cups corn kernels
    for popcorn
10ml/2 tsp mild or hot chilli powder
juice of 2 limes

1 Heat the oil in a large, heavy frying pan until it is very hot. Add the popcorn and immediately cover the pan with a lid and reduce the heat.

2 After a few minutes, the corn should start to pop. Resist the temptation to lift the lid to check. Shake the pan occasionally so that all the corn will be cooked and lightly browned.

3 When the sound of popping corn has stopped, quickly remove the pan from the heat and allow to cool slightly. Take off the lid and use a spoon to lift out and discard any corn kernels that have not popped. Any uncooked corn will have fallen to the base of the pan and will be inedible.

4 Add the chilli powder to the pan. Replace the lid firmly and shake the pan repeatedly to make sure that all of the corn is covered with a colourful dusting of chilli powder.

5 Tip the popcorn into a large bowl and keep warm. Sprinkle over the juice of the limes immediately prior to serving the popcorn.

Dips and snacks may whet the appetite, but it's the first

course that really determines whether a meal will go

with a swing. Play safe with a humdrum appetizer, and

you set the scene for a staid and sensible evening;

introduce chillies and there's no telling what could

happen. Whether you select a soup with a teasing

warmth that keeps everyone guessing as to its source,

or make a more blatant statement with something like

Caribbean Chilli Crab Cakes, conversation — and

compliments — will flow like wine.

Soups and Appetizers

HOT <u>AND</u> SPICY MISO BROTH <u>WITH</u> TOFU

THE JAPANESE EAT MISO BROTH, A SIMPLE BUT HIGHLY NUTRITIOUS SOUP, ALMOST EVERY DAY — IT IS STANDARD BREAKFAST FARE AND IT IS EATEN WITH RICE OR NOODLES LATER IN THE DAY.

SERVES FOUR

INGREDIENTS

   1 bunch of spring onions (scallions)
     or 5 baby leeks
   15g/½oz/⅓ cup fresh
     coriander (cilantro)
   3 thin slices fresh root ginger
   2 star anise
   1 small dried red chilli
   1.2 litres/2 pints/5 cups dashi stock
     or vegetable stock
   225g/8oz pak choi (bok choy) or
     other Asian greens, thickly sliced
   200g/7oz firm tofu, cut into
     2.5cm/1in squares
   45–60ml/3–4 tbsp red miso
   30–45ml/2–3 tbsp Japanese soy
     sauce (shoyu)
   1 fresh red chilli, seeded
     and shredded

1 Cut the coarse green tops off half of the spring onions or leeks and place in a pan with the coriander stalks, ginger, star anise and dried chilli. Pour in the dashi or vegetable stock. Heat gently until boiling, then simmer for 10 minutes. Strain, return to the pan and reheat until simmering.

2 Slice the remaining spring onions or leeks finely on the diagonal and add the green portion to the soup with the pak choi or greens and squares of tofu. Cook for 2 minutes.

3 Mix 45ml/3 tbsp of the miso with a little of the hot soup in a bowl, then stir it into the soup. Taste the soup and add more miso with soy sauce to taste.

4 Coarsely chop the coriander leaves and stir most of them into the soup with the white part of the spring onions or leeks. Cook for 1 minute, then ladle the soup into heated serving bowls. Sprinkle with the remaining chopped coriander and the shredded fresh red chilli and serve immediately.

COOK'S TIPS
• Dashi powder is available in most Asian and Chinese stores. Alternatively, make your own by gently simmering 10–15cm/ 4–6in kombu seaweed in 1.2 litres/ 2 pints/5 cups water for 10 minutes. Do not boil the stock vigorously as this would make the dashi bitter. Remove the kombu, then add 15g/½oz dried bonito flakes and bring to the boil. Strain immediately through a fine sieve.
• Kombu seaweed is usually dried, pickled or shaved thinly in dry sheets. Wash dried kombu before using.
• Red miso is a paste made from fermented beans and grains. Buy it from Asian food stores. It will keep almost indefinitely in an airtight container in the refrigerator.

PROVENÇAL FISH SOUP WITH ROUILLE

AN AUTHENTIC CHILLI-SPIKED ROUILLE LIFTS THIS EXCELLENT SOUP INTO THE REALMS OF THE SUBLIME. A GOOD SOUP FOR A PARTY BECAUSE YOU CAN PREPARE IT ALL IN ADVANCE.

SERVES FOUR TO SIX

INGREDIENTS
   30ml/2 tbsp olive oil
   1 leek, sliced
   2 celery sticks, chopped
   1 onion, chopped
   2 garlic cloves, chopped
   4 ripe tomatoes, chopped
   15ml/1 tbsp tomato purée (paste)
   150ml/¼ pint/⅔ cup dry white wine
   1 bay leaf
   5ml/1 tsp saffron threads
   fish trimmings, bones and heads
   1kg/2¼lb mixed fish fillets and
      prepared shellfish
   salt and ground black pepper
   croûtons and grated Gruyère cheese,
      to serve
For the rouille
   1 slice of white bread,
      crusts removed
   1 red (bell) pepper, cored, seeded
      and quartered
   1–2 fresh red chillies, seeded
      and chopped
   2 garlic cloves, roughly chopped
   olive oil (optional)

1 Make the rouille. Soak the bread in 30–45ml/2–3 tbsp cold water for 10 minutes. Meanwhile, grill (broil) the red pepper, skin side up, until the skin is charred and blistered. Put into a plastic bag and tie the top to keep the steam in. Leave until cool enough to handle. Peel off the skin. Drain the bread and squeeze out excess water.

2 Roughly chop the pepper quarters and place in a blender or food processor with the bread, chillies and garlic. Process to a fairly coarse paste, adding a little olive oil, if necessary. Scrape the rouille into a small bowl and set it aside.

COOK'S TIP
If you are preparing this soup in advance, cook it for the time stated then cool and chill as rapidly as possible. A fish soup should not be left simmering on top of the stove.

3 Heat the olive oil in a large pan. Add the leek, celery, onion and garlic. Cook gently for 10 minutes until soft. Add the tomatoes, tomato purée, wine, bay leaf, saffron and the fish trimmings. Bring to the boil, reduce the heat, cover and simmer for 30 minutes.

4 Strain through a colander into a clean pan, pressing out all the liquid. Cut the fish fillets into large chunks and add to the liquid, with the shellfish. Cover and simmer for 5–10 minutes until cooked.

5 Strain through a colander into a clean pan. Put half the cooked fish into a blender or food processor with about 300ml/½ pint/1¼ cups of the soup. Process for just long enough to blend, while retaining some texture.

6 Stir the processed mixture back into the remaining soup, then add the fish and shellfish from the colander, with salt and pepper to taste. Reheat gently. Serve the soup with the rouille, croûtons and cheese.

THAI CHICKEN AND CHILLI SOUP

THIS AROMATIC SOUP IS RICH WITH COCONUT MILK AND INTENSELY FLAVOURED WITH GALANGAL, WHICH IS MILDLY PEPPERY AND GINGERY, TOGETHER WITH LEMON GRASS AND KAFFIR LIME LEAVES.

SERVES FOUR TO SIX

INGREDIENTS

    4 lemon grass stalks, trimmed and
      outer leaves discarded
    2 × 400ml/14fl oz/1⅔ cup cans
      coconut milk
    475ml/16fl oz/2 cups chicken stock
    2.5cm/1in piece galangal
    2 fresh red chillies
    10 black peppercorns, crushed
    10 kaffir lime leaves, torn
    300g/11oz skinless, boneless chicken
      breast portions, cut into thin strips
    115g/4oz/1½ cups button
      (white) mushrooms
    50g/2oz/½ cup baby corn cobs,
      quartered lengthways
    60ml/4 tbsp lime juice
    45ml/3 tbsp Thai fish sauce (*nam pla*)
    chopped spring onions (scallions)
      and fresh coriander (cilantro)
      leaves, to garnish

1 Cut off the lower 5cm/2in from each lemon grass stalk and chop it finely. Bruise the remaining pieces of stalk. Bring the coconut milk and chicken stock to the boil in a large pan. Peel and thinly slice the galangal. Seed and finely chop the chillies. Add all the lemon grass, the galangal and half the chopped chillies, then stir in the peppercorns and half the lime leaves, lower the heat and simmer gently for 10 minutes. Strain into a clean pan.

2 Return the soup to the heat, then add the chicken, mushrooms and the quartered baby corn cobs. Bring to the boil, then lower the heat and simmer for 5–7 minutes or until the chicken is cooked.

3 Stir in the lime juice and fish sauce, then add the remaining lime leaves. Serve hot, garnished with the remaining chopped chillies and the spring onions and coriander.

HOT-AND-SOUR SHELLFISH SOUP

THIS IS A CLASSIC THAI SHELLFISH SOUP – TOM YAM KUNG. THE BALANCE OF FLAVOURS IS WHAT COUNTS, SO YOU MAY WANT TO START WITH HALF THE CHILLIES AND ADD MORE TO TASTE.

SERVES FOUR TO SIX

INGREDIENTS

    450g/1lb raw king prawns (jumbo
      shrimp), thawed if frozen
    1 litre/1¾ pints/4 cups chicken stock
      or water
    3 lemon grass stalks, trimmed
    10 kaffir lime leaves, torn in half
    225g/8oz can straw mushrooms
    45ml/3 tbsp Thai fish sauce
      (*nam pla*)
    60ml/4 tbsp lime juice
    30ml/2 tbsp chopped spring
      onion (scallion)
    15ml/1 tbsp fresh coriander
      (cilantro) leaves
    4 fresh red chillies, seeded and
      thinly sliced
    salt and ground black pepper

1 Shell the prawns, putting the shells in a colander. Devein the prawns and set them aside. Rinse the shells under cold water, drain, then put in a large pan with the stock or water. Bring to the boil.

2 Bruise the lemon grass stalks and add them to the stock with half the lime leaves. Simmer gently for 5–6 minutes.

3 Strain the stock, return it to the clean pan and reheat. Drain the straw mushrooms and add them with the prawns. Cook until the prawns turn pink. Stir in the fish sauce, lime juice, spring onion, coriander, chillies and the remaining lime leaves. Taste and adjust the seasoning. The soup should be sour, salty, spicy and hot.

SPICY PEANUT BALLS

TASTY RICE BALLS, ROLLED IN CHOPPED PEANUTS AND DEEP-FRIED, MAKE A DELICIOUS SNACK. SERVE THEM AS THEY ARE OR WITH A CHILLI SAUCE FOR DIPPING.

2 Add three-quarters of the cooked rice to the paste in the food processor, and process until smooth and sticky. Scrape into a mixing bowl and stir in the remainder of the rice. Wet your hands and shape the mixture into small balls.

3 Roll the balls, a few at a time, in the chopped peanuts, making sure they are evenly coated.

4 Heat the oil for deep-frying to 180–190ºC/350–375ºF or until a cube of day-old bread browns in about 45 seconds. Deep-fry the peanut balls until crisp. Drain on kitchen paper, then pile on to a platter. Serve hot with lime wedges and a chilli dipping sauce, if you like.

MAKES SIXTEEN

INGREDIENTS
- 1 garlic clove, crushed
- 1cm/½in piece of fresh root ginger, peeled and finely chopped
- 1 small fresh red chilli, seeded and roughly chopped
- 1.5ml/¼ tsp ground turmeric
- 5ml/1 tsp granulated sugar
- 2.5ml/½ tsp salt
- 5ml/1 tsp chilli sauce
- 10ml/2 tsp soy sauce
- 30ml/2 tbsp chopped fresh coriander (cilantro)
- juice of ½ lime
- 225g/8oz/2 cups cooked white long grain rice
- 115g/4oz/1 cup peanuts, chopped
- vegetable oil, for deep-frying
- lime wedges and chilli dipping sauce, to serve (optional)

1 Put the crushed garlic, ginger and chilli in a food processor. Add the turmeric and process to a paste. Add the granulated sugar, salt, chilli sauce and soy sauce, with the chopped coriander and lime juice. Process briefly to mix.

COOK'S TIP
Coat the balls in the peanuts and then chill for 30 minutes before deep-frying.

CARIBBEAN CHILLI CRAB CAKES

CRAB MEAT MAKES WONDERFUL FISH CAKES, AS EVIDENCED WITH THESE GUTSY MORSELS. THE RICH, SPICY TOMATO DIP IS DELICIOUS, BUT YOU COULD ALSO SERVE A FRESH TOMATO AND CHILLI SALSA.

MAKES ABOUT FIFTEEN

INGREDIENTS
  225g/8oz white crab meat (fresh,
    frozen or canned)
  115g/4oz cooked floury
    potatoes, mashed
  30ml/2 tbsp fresh herb seasoning
  2.5ml/½ tsp mild mustard
  2.5ml/½ tsp ground black pepper
  ½ fresh hot chilli, seeded and
    finely chopped
  5ml/1 tsp chopped fresh oregano
  1 egg, beaten
  plain (all-purpose) flour,
    for dredging
  vegetable oil, for frying
  lime wedges, coriander (cilantro)
    sprigs and fresh whole chillies,
    to garnish
For the tomato dip
  15g/½oz/1 tbsp butter
  ½ onion, finely chopped
  2 drained canned plum
    tomatoes, chopped
  1 garlic clove, crushed
  150ml/¼ pint/⅔ cup water
  5–10ml/1–2 tsp malt vinegar
  15ml/1 tbsp chopped fresh
    coriander (cilantro)
  ½ fresh chilli, seeded and chopped

1 To make the crab cakes, mix the crab meat, potatoes, herb seasoning, mustard, pepper, chilli, oregano and egg in a large bowl. Chill the mixture in the bowl for at least 30 minutes.

COOK'S TIP
Use French Dijon mustard for this dish as it is not as overpowering as English.

2 Meanwhile, make the tomato dip. Melt the butter in a small pan and sauté the onion, tomatoes and garlic for about 5 minutes until the onion is tender. Add the water, vinegar, coriander and fresh chilli. Bring to the boil, then reduce the heat and simmer for 10 minutes.

3 Pour the mixture into a blender or food processor and blend to a smooth purée. Scrape into a pan or bowl. Keep warm or chill.

4 Preheat the oven. Using a spoon, shape the crab mixture into rounds and dredge with flour, shaking off the excess. Heat a little oil in a frying pan and fry, a few at a time, for 2–3 minutes on each side. Drain the crab cakes on kitchen paper and keep warm in a low oven while cooking the remainder.

5 Garnish with lime wedges, coriander sprigs and whole chillies. Serve with the tomato dip.

CHILLI SPICED ONION KOFTAS

THESE DELICIOUS DEEP-FRIED INDIAN ONION FRITTERS ARE PEPPED UP WITH GREEN CHILLIES.
SERVE THEM WITH A YOGURT DIP, TO DAMP DOWN THEIR FIRE.

SERVES FOUR TO FIVE

INGREDIENTS
    675g/1½lb onions, halved and
        thinly sliced
    5ml/1 tsp salt
    5ml/1 tsp ground coriander
    5ml/1 tsp ground cumin
    2.5ml/½ tsp ground turmeric
    1–2 fresh green chillies, seeded and
        finely chopped
    45ml/3 tbsp chopped fresh
        coriander (cilantro)
    90g/3½oz/¾ cup chickpea flour
    2.5ml/½ tsp baking powder
    vegetable oil, for deep-frying
To serve
    lemon wedges
    fresh coriander (cilantro) sprigs
    yogurt and herb dip (see Cook's Tips)

1 Put the onion slices in a colander, add the salt and toss well. Stand the colander on a plate or bowl and leave for 45 minutes, tossing once or twice with a fork. Rinse the onions, then squeeze out the excess moisture. Tip the onions into a bowl. Add the ground coriander, cumin, turmeric, chillies and fresh coriander. Mix well.

COOK'S TIPS
• Chickpea flour, available from supermarkets and Indian food stores, is sometimes labelled gram flour or *besan*.
• To make a yogurt and herb dip, stir 30ml/2 tbsp each of chopped fresh coriander (cilantro) and mint into 250ml/8fl oz/1 cup thick yogurt. Add salt, ground toasted cumin seeds and a pinch of sugar. Top with a chopped chilli.

2 Add the chickpea flour and baking powder, then use your hand to mix all the ingredients thoroughly.

3 Shape the mixture by hand into 12–15 koftas. They should be about the size of golf balls.

4 Heat the oil for deep-frying to 180–190ºC/350–375ºF or until a cube of day-old bread browns in about 45 seconds.

5 Fry the koftas, 4–5 at a time, until deep golden brown all over. Drain each batch on kitchen paper and keep warm until all the koftas are cooked. Serve with lemon wedges, coriander sprigs and a yogurt and herb dip.

SPRING ROLLS WITH FIERY CHILLI SAUCE

THIS POPULAR SNACK COMES FROM SOUTH-EAST ASIA, AND WOULD MAKE A TASTY FIRST COURSE. THE SAUCE IS TRADITIONALLY MADE WITH HOT CHILLIES, BUT SUBSTITUTE MILDER ONES, IF YOU PREFER.

SERVES FOUR TO SIX

INGREDIENTS
25g/1oz cellophane noodles soaked
  for 10 minutes in hot water to cover
6–8 dried wood ears, soaked for
  30 minutes in warm water to cover
225g/8oz minced (ground) pork
225g/8oz fresh or canned crab meat
4 spring onions (scallions),
  finely chopped
5ml/1 tsp Thai fish sauce (*nam pla*)
250g/9oz packet spring roll wrappers
flour and water paste, to seal
vegetable oil, for deep-frying
salt and ground black pepper
For the sauce
2 fresh red chillies, seeded
2 garlic cloves, chopped
15ml/1 tbsp granulated sugar
45ml/3 tbsp Thai fish sauce
  (*nam pla*)
juice of 1 lime or ½ lemon

2 Mix the noodles and the wood ears with the pork and set aside. Remove any cartilage from the crab meat and add to the pork mixture with the spring onions and Thai fish sauce. Season to taste, mixing well.

3 Place a spring roll wrapper in front of you, diamond-fashion. Spoon some mixture just below the centre, across the width, fold over the nearest point and roll once.

4 Fold in the sides to enclose the mixture, then brush the edges with flour paste and roll up to seal. Repeat with the remaining spring roll wrappers and filling mixture.

5 Heat the oil in a wok or deep-fryer to 190°C/375°F. Deep-fry the rolls in batches for 8–10 minutes or until they are cooked through. Drain them well on kitchen paper and serve hot. To eat, dip the rolls in the fiery chilli sauce.

1 Make the sauce by pounding the chillies and garlic to a paste. Scrape into a bowl and mix in the sugar and fish sauce, with citrus juice to taste. Drain the noodles and snip them into 2.5cm/1in lengths. Drain the wood ears, trim away any rough stems and slice the caps finely. Mix with the noodles.

COOK'S TIPS
• Wood ears (Chinese black fungus) is a gelatinous species collected and cultivated in China.
• Serve the rolls Vietnamese-style by wrapping each one in a lettuce leaf with a few sprigs of fresh mint and coriander (cilantro) and a stick of cucumber.

PEPPERS <u>WITH</u> CHEESE <u>AND</u> CHILLI FILLING

SWEET PEPPERS AND CHILLIES ARE NATURAL COMPANIONS, SO IT ISN'T SURPRISING THAT THEY WORK SO WELL TOGETHER IN THIS TRADITIONAL BULGARIAN APPETIZER OR LIGHT SNACK.

3 Using a sharp knife, carefully peel away the skin from the peppers.

4 Beat together all the ingredients for the filling in a bowl. Divide evenly among the 4 peppers.

5 Reshape the peppers to look whole. Dip them into the seasoned flour, then in the egg and then the flour again.

6 Heat the olive oil for shallow frying in a large pan and fry the peeled peppers gently for 6–8 minutes, turning once with a spatula, until they are golden brown and the filling is set. Drain the peppers thoroughly on kitchen paper before serving with a cucumber and tomato salad.

SERVES TWO TO FOUR

INGREDIENTS
  4 red, yellow or green sweet peppers,
    either bell peppers or long peppers
  50g/2oz/½ cup plain (all-purpose)
    flour, seasoned
  1 egg, beaten
  olive oil, for shallow frying
  cucumber and tomato salad,
    to serve
For the filling
  1 egg
  90g/3½oz/generous ½ cup finely
    crumbled feta cheese
  30ml/2 tbsp chopped fresh parsley
  1 small fresh red or green chilli,
    seeded and finely chopped

1 Preheat the grill (broiler). Slit open the peppers lengthways on one side only, enabling you to scoop out the seeds and remove the cores, but leaving them in one piece.

2 Place the peppers in a grill (broiling) pan. Cook under medium heat until the skin is charred and blackened. Place the peppers in a plastic bag, tie the top to keep the steam in and set aside for 20 minutes.

COOK'S TIP
Feta cheese should have a bland, salt-edged taste. If kept in brine for some time it will be saltier and may need to be first soaked in water.

PRAWN FRITTERS <u>WITH</u> CHILLI DIPPING SAUCE

THESE DELECTABLE FRITTERS COME FROM THE PHILIPPINES. UNUSUALLY, THEY ARE FIRST SHALLOW FRIED, THEN DEEP-FRIED. EAT THEM FRESH FROM THE PAN, DIPPED IN THE PIQUANT SAUCE.

SERVES TWO TO FOUR

INGREDIENTS
    16 raw prawns (shrimp),
      in the shell
    225g/8oz/2 cups plain
      (all-purpose) flour
    5ml/1 tsp baking powder
    2.5ml/½ tsp salt
    1 egg, beaten
    1 small sweet potato
    1 garlic clove, crushed
    115g/4oz/2 cups beansprouts,
      soaked in cold water for
      10 minutes and well drained
    vegetable oil, for shallow and
      deep-frying
    4 spring onions
      (scallions), chopped
For the dipping sauce
    1 jumbo garlic clove, sliced
    45ml/3 tbsp rice or
      wine vinegar
    15–30ml/1–2 tbsp water
    salt, to taste
    6–8 small fresh red chillies

1 Mix together all the 5 ingredients for the dipping sauce and divide between 2–4 small wide bowls. The garlic slices and whole chillies will float on top.

2 Put the prawns in a pan with cold water to cover. Bring to the boil, reduce the heat and then simmer for about 4–5 minutes or until the prawns are pink and tender when pierced with the tip of a sharp knife. Lift them out with a slotted spoon and drain well. Discard the heads and the body shell, but leave the tails on. Strain and reserve the cooking liquid. Set aside and leave to cool.

VARIATIONS
• Use cooked tiger prawns (jumbo shrimp) if you prefer. In this case, make the batter using ready-made fish stock or chicken stock.
• You could substitute 15ml/1 tbsp very finely sliced fresh ginger for the garlic in the dipping sauce, if you like.

3 Sift the flour, baking powder and salt into a bowl. Add the beaten egg and about 300ml/½ pint/1¼ cups of the reserved prawn stock and beat to make a batter that has the consistency of double (heavy) cream.

4 Peel the sweet potato and grate it coarsely. Add it to the batter, then stir in the crushed garlic. Pat the beansprouts dry in kitchen paper and add to the batter.

5 Pour the oil for shallow frying into a large frying pan. It should be about 5mm/¼in deep. Pour more oil into a wok for deep-frying. Heat the oil in the frying pan. Taking a generous spoonful of the batter, drop it carefully into the frying pan so that it spreads out to a fritter about 10cm/4in across.

6 Add more batter to the pan but do not let the fritters touch. As soon as the fritters have set, top each one with a single prawn and a few pieces of chopped spring onion. Continue to cook over a medium heat for 1 minute, then remove with a spatula.

7 Heat the oil in the wok to 190°C/375°F and deep-fry the fritters in batches until they are crisp and golden brown. Drain on kitchen paper and then arrange on a serving plate or platter. Serve with the dipping sauce.

CHILLI CRABS

EAT THESE CRABS SINGAPOREAN STYLE, WITH THE FINGERS. GIVE GUESTS CRAB CRACKERS FOR THE CLAWS AND HAVE SOME FINGER BOWLS OR HOT TOWELS TO HAND AS THE MEAL WILL BE MESSY.

SERVES FOUR

INGREDIENTS

2 cooked crabs, each about
  675g/1½lb
90ml/6 tbsp sunflower oil
2.5cm/1in piece fresh root ginger,
  peeled and chopped
2–3 garlic cloves, crushed
1–2 fresh red chillies, seeded and
  pounded to a paste
175ml/6fl oz/¾ cup tomato ketchup
30ml/2 tbsp soft light brown sugar
15ml/1 tbsp light soy sauce
120ml/4fl oz/½ cup boiling water
salt
hot toast and cucumber chunks,
  to serve

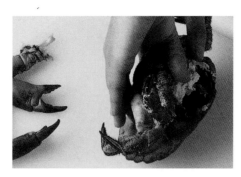

1 Prepare each crab in turn. Twist off the large claws, then turn the crab on its back with its mouth and eyes facing away from you. Using both of your thumbs, push the body, with the small legs attached, upwards from beneath the flap, separating the body from the main shell in the process. Discard the stomach sac and grey spongy lungs.

2 Using a teaspoon, scrape the brown creamy meat from the large shell into a small bowl. Twist the legs from the body. Cut the body section in half. Pick out the white meat and add it to the bowl. Pick out the meat from the legs, or leave it for guests to remove at the table.

3 Heat the oil in a wok and gently fry the ginger, garlic and fresh chilli paste for 1–2 minutes without browning. Stir in the ketchup, sugar and soy sauce, with salt to taste and heat gently.

4 Stir in all the crab meat. Pour in the boiling water, stir well and heat through over a high heat. Pile on serving plates. If the crab claws were left intact, add them to the plate, with the cucumber. Serve immediately, with pieces of toast.

NONYA PORK SATAY

THERE ARE FEW DISHES AS DELICIOUS AS SATAY. THE SKEWERS OF SPICED MEAT CAN BE SERVED AS SNACKS, AS PART OF A BARBECUE OR AS A LIGHT MEAL.

SERVES EIGHT TO TWELVE

INGREDIENTS

450g/1lb pork fillet (tenderloin)
15ml/1 tbsp soft light brown sugar
1cm/½in cube shrimp paste
1–2 lemon grass stalks, trimmed
30ml/2 tbsp coriander
  seeds, dry-fried
6 macadamia nuts or blanched almonds
2 onions, roughly chopped
3–6 fresh red chillies, seeded and
  roughly chopped
2.5ml/½ tsp ground turmeric
300ml/½ pint/1¼ cups canned
  coconut milk
30ml/2 tbsp groundnut (peanut) oil
  or sunflower oil
salt

COOK'S TIP
How many chillies you use for the marinade depends on their strength.

1 Soak 8–12 bamboo skewers in water for at least 1 hour to prevent them from scorching when they are placed under the grill (broiler).

2 Cut the pork into small chunks, then spread it out in a single layer in a shallow dish. Sprinkle with the sugar to help release the juices. Wrap the shrimp paste in foil and heat it briefly in a dry frying pan or warm it on a skewer held over a gas flame.

3 Cut off the lower 5cm/2in of the lemon grass stalks and chop finely. Process the dry-fried coriander seeds to a powder in a food processor. Add the nuts and chopped lemon grass, process briefly, then add the onions, chillies, shrimp paste, turmeric and a little salt; process to a fine paste. Pour in the coconut milk and oil. Switch the machine on very briefly to mix.

4 Pour the mixture over the pork, stir well, cover and leave to marinate for 1–2 hours.

5 Preheat the grill or prepare the barbecue. Drain the bamboo skewers and thread 3–4 pieces of marinated pork on each. Cook the skewered meat for 8–10 minutes, turning often until tender and basting frequently with the remaining marinade. Serve as soon as they are cooked.

Some people find fish a little on the bland side, but there's no danger of that with the exciting ideas you'll find in this chapter. Fish and Coconut Curry, from Malaysia, is a deliciously aromatic dish, while Cajun Blackened Fish with Papaya Salsa is a fiery and flavoursome method of frying any fish of your choice, originating in Louisiana in the southern USA. In Fish and Shellfish Laksa, the heat is tempered by the addition of rice noodles and coconut milk, while rice performs a similar function in the delectable Louisiana Shellfish Gumbo.

Fish and Shellfish Dishes

CAJUN BLACKENED FISH WITH PAPAYA SALSA

THIS IS AN EXCELLENT WAY OF COOKING FILLETS OF SNAPPER OR COD, LEAVING IT MOIST IN THE MIDDLE AND CRISP AND SPICY ON THE OUTSIDE.

SERVES FOUR

INGREDIENTS
   5ml/1 tsp black peppercorns
   5ml/1 tsp cumin seeds
   5ml/1 tsp white mustard seeds
   10ml/2 tsp paprika
   5ml/1 tsp chilli powder
   5ml/1 tsp dried oregano
   10ml/2 tsp dried thyme
   4 skinned fish fillets, 225g/8oz each
   50g/2oz/¼ cup butter, melted
   salt
   lime wedges and coriander (cilantro)
      sprigs, to garnish
For the papaya salsa
   1 papaya
   1 fresh red chilli
   ½ small red onion, diced
   45ml/3 tbsp chopped fresh
      coriander (cilantro)
   grated rind and juice of 1 lime

1 Start by making the salsa. Cut the papaya in half and scoop out the seeds. Remove the skin, cut the flesh into small dice and place it in a bowl. Slit the chilli, remove and discard the seeds and finely chop the flesh.

2 Add the onion, chilli, coriander, lime rind and juice to the papaya. Season with salt to taste. Mix well and set aside.

3 Dry-fry the peppercorns, cumin and mustard seeds in a pan, then grind them to a fine powder. Add the paprika, chilli powder, oregano, thyme and 5ml/1 tsp salt. Grind again and spread on a plate.

4 Preheat a heavy frying pan over a medium heat for about 10 minutes. Brush the fish fillets with the melted butter then dip them in the spices until well coated.

5 Place the fish in the hot pan and cook for 1–2 minutes on each side until blackened. Garnish with lime and coriander, and serve with the salsa.

COOK'S TIP
Cooking fish in this way can be a smoky affair, so make sure the kitchen is well ventilated or use an extractor fan.

CARIBBEAN FISH STEAKS

THIS QUICK AND EASY RECIPE IS A GOOD EXAMPLE OF HOW CHILLIES, CAYENNE AND ALLSPICE CAN ADD AN EXOTIC ACCENT TO A TOMATO SAUCE FOR FISH.

SERVES FOUR

INGREDIENTS
   4 cod steaks
   5ml/1 tsp muscovado
      (molasses) sugar
   10ml/2 tsp angostura bitters
   salt
   steamed okra or green beans,
   to serve
For the tomato sauce
   45ml/3 tbsp oil
   6 shallots, finely chopped
   1 garlic clove, crushed
   1 fresh green chilli, seeded and
      finely chopped
   400g/14oz can chopped tomatoes
   2 bay leaves
   1.5ml/¼ tsp cayenne pepper
   5ml/1 tsp crushed allspice
   juice of 2 limes

1 First make the tomato sauce. Heat the oil in a frying pan and fry the shallots, until soft. Add the garlic and chilli, and cook for 2 minutes. Stir in the tomatoes, bay, cayenne, allspice and lime juice, with salt to taste.

VARIATION
Almost any robust fish steaks or fillets can be cooked in this way.

2 Cook gently for 15 minutes, then add the cod steaks and baste with the tomato sauce. Cover and cook for 10 minutes or until the cod steaks are cooked. Keep hot in a warmed dish.

3 Stir the sugar and angostura bitters into the sauce, simmer for 2 minutes, then pour it over the fish. Serve with steamed okra or green beans.

SWORDFISH TACOS

COOKED CORRECTLY, SWORDFISH IS MOIST AND MEATY, AND SUFFICIENTLY ROBUST TO MORE THAN HOLD ITS OWN WHEN MIXED WITH CHILLIES. IT MAKES A VERY TASTY FILLING FOR TACOS.

SERVES SIX

INGREDIENTS

3 swordfish steaks
30ml/2 tbsp vegetable oil
2 garlic cloves, crushed
1 small onion, chopped
3 fresh green chillies, seeded
  and chopped
3 tomatoes
small bunch of fresh coriander
  (cilantro), chopped
6 fresh corn tortillas
½ Iceberg lettuce, shredded
salt and ground black pepper
lemon wedges, to serve (optional)

1 Preheat the grill (broiler). Put the swordfish on an oiled rack over a grill (broiling) pan and grill (broil) for no longer than 2–3 minutes on each side. When cool, remove the skin and flake the fish into a bowl.

2 Heat the oil in a pan and gently fry the crushed garlic, and chopped onion and chillies for 5 minutes or until the onion is soft.

3 Cut a cross in the base of each tomato. Put them in a heatproof bowl and pour over boiling water. After 30 seconds, plunge into cold water. Drain and remove the skins. Cut them in half and squeeze out the seeds and dice the flesh.

4 Add the tomatoes and swordfish to the onion mixture. Cook for 5 minutes over a low heat. Add the coriander and cook for 1–2 minutes. Season to taste with salt and pepper.

5 Wrap the tortillas in foil and steam on a plate over boiling water until pliable. Place some shredded lettuce and fish mixture on each tortilla. Fold in half and serve immediately, with lemon wedges if you like.

SWORDFISH WITH CHILLI AND LIME SAUCE

SWORDFISH IS A PRIME CANDIDATE FOR THE BARBECUE, AS LONG AS IT IS NOT OVERCOOKED. IT TASTES WONDERFUL WITH A SPICY SAUCE WHOSE FIRE IS TEMPERED WITH CRÈME FRAÎCHE.

SERVES FOUR

INGREDIENTS

2 fresh serrano chillies
4 tomatoes
45ml/3 tbsp olive oil
grated rind and juice of
  1 lime
4 swordfish steaks
2.5ml/½ tsp salt
2.5ml/½ tsp ground black pepper
175ml/6fl oz/¾ cup crème fraîche
fresh flat leaf parsley, to garnish

1 Roast the chillies in a dry griddle pan until the skins are blistered. Put in a plastic bag and tie the top. Set aside for 20 minutes, then peel off the skins. Cut off the stalks, then slit the chillies, scrape out the seeds and slice the flesh.

2 Cut a cross in the base of each tomato. Place them in a heatproof bowl and pour over boiling water to cover. After 30 seconds, lift the tomatoes out on a slotted spoon and plunge them into a bowl of cold water. Drain. The skins will have begun to peel back from the crosses. Remove the skin from the tomatoes, then cut them in half and squeeze out the seeds. Chop the flesh into 1cm/½in pieces.

3 Heat 15ml/1 tbsp of the oil in a small pan and add the strips of chilli, with the lime rind and juice. Cook for 2–3 minutes, then stir in the tomatoes. Cook for 10 minutes, stirring the mixture occasionally, until the tomato is pulpy. Preheat the grill (broiler) or prepare the barbecue.

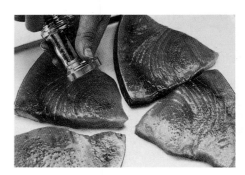

4 Brush the swordfish steaks with olive oil and season. Cook on the barbecue or grill (broil) for 3–4 minutes or until just cooked, turning once. Meanwhile, stir the crème fraîche into the sauce and heat it through gently. Pour over the swordfish steaks. Serve garnished with fresh parsley. This is delicious served with chargrilled vegetables.

STEAMED FISH WITH CHILLI SAUCE

CHILLIES CAN BE USED IN MANY DIFFERENT WAYS. HERE THEY FLAVOUR A WHOLE FISH SIMPLY BY BEING STREWN OVER DURING STEAMING. AN EXTRA KICK COMES FROM THE HOT SAUCE.

SERVES FOUR

INGREDIENTS
   1 large, firm fish such as bass or
     grouper, scaled and cleaned
   1 fresh banana leaf or piece of foil
   2 lemon grass stalks, trimmed
   30ml/2 tbsp rice wine
   3 fresh red chillies, seeded and
     finely sliced
   2 garlic cloves, finely chopped
   2cm/¾in piece fresh root ginger,
     finely shredded
   2 spring onions (scallions), chopped
   30ml/2 tbsp Thai fish sauce (*nam pla*)
   juice of 1 lime
For the hot chilli sauce
   10 fresh red chillies, seeded and
     roughly chopped
   4 garlic cloves, halved
   60ml/4 tbsp Thai fish sauce
    (*nam pla*)
   15ml/1 tbsp granulated sugar
   75ml/5 tbsp lime juice

1 Rinse the fish under cold running water. Pat dry with kitchen paper. With a sharp knife, slash the skin of the fish a few times on both sides.

2 Place the fish on a banana leaf or a piece of foil. Cut off the lower 5cm/2in of the lemon grass and chop it finely. Put it in a bowl, stir in all the remaining ingredients and spoon the mixture over the fish.

COOK'S TIP
Ten chillies may seem a lot for the sauce, but bear in mind that the mixture is meant to be used sparingly.

3 Place a rack or a small upturned plate in the base of a wok and pour in boiling water to a depth of 5cm/2in. Lift the banana leaf or piece of foil holding the fish, and place on the rack or plate (the water should not come into contact with the fish). Cover with a lid and steam for about 10–15 minutes or until the fish is cooked through.

4 Place all the chilli sauce ingredients in a food processor and process until smooth. You may need to add a little cold water. Scrape into a bowl.

5 Serve the fish hot, on the banana leaf if you like, with the chilli sauce to spoon sparingly over the top. This dish goes very well with boiled rice or potatoes.

FISH <u>AND</u> COCONUT CURRY

THIS IS A WONDERFULLY AROMATIC SOUTH-EAST ASIAN CURRY. CHOOSE A FIRM-TEXTURED FISH SO THAT THE PIECES STAY INTACT DURING THE BRIEF COOKING PROCESS.

SERVES FOUR

INGREDIENTS

500g/1¼lb firm-textured fish fillets, skinned and cut into 2.5cm/ 1in cubes
2.5ml/½ tsp salt
50g/2oz/⅔ cup desiccated (dry unsweetened shredded) coconut
6 shallots or small onions, roughly chopped
6 blanched almonds
2–3 garlic cloves, roughly chopped
2.5cm/1in piece fresh root ginger, peeled and sliced
2 lemon grass stalks, trimmed
10ml/2 tsp ground turmeric
45ml/3 tbsp vegetable oil
2 × 400ml/14fl oz cans coconut milk
1–3 fresh red or green chillies, seeded and sliced
salt and ground black pepper
fresh chives, to garnish
boiled long grain rice, to serve

1 Spread out the pieces of fish in a shallow dish and sprinkle them with the salt. Dry-fry the coconut in a wok over medium to low heat, turning all the time until it is crisp and golden (see Cook's Tip below).

2 Tip the dry-fried coconut into a food processor and process until you have an oily paste. Scrape into a bowl and reserve.

3 Add the shallots or onions, almonds, garlic and ginger to the food processor. Cut off the lower 5cm/2in of the lemon grass stalks, chop them roughly and add to the other ingredients in the processor. Process the mixture to a paste. Bruise the remaining lemon grass and set the stalks aside.

4 Add the ground turmeric to the mixture in the processor and process briefly to mix.

5 Heat the oil in the clean wok. Add the onion mixture and cook for a few minutes without browning. Stir in the coconut milk and bring to the boil, stirring constantly to prevent the mixture from curdling.

6 Add the cubes of fish, most of the sliced chillies and the bruised lemon grass stalks. Cook for 3–4 minutes. Stir in the coconut paste (moistened with some of the sauce if necessary) and cook for a further 2–3 minutes only. Do not overcook the fish. Taste and adjust the seasoning.

7 Remove the lemon grass stalks. Spoon the moolie on to a hot serving dish and sprinkle with the remaining slices of chilli. Garnish with chopped and whole chives and serve with boiled long grain rice.

COOK'S TIP
Dry-frying is a feature of Malay cooking that demands the cook's close attention. The coconut must be constantly on the move so that it becomes crisp and uniformly golden in colour.

LOUISIANA SHELLFISH GUMBO

GUMBO IS A SOUP, BUT IS SERVED OVER RICE AS A MAIN COURSE. IN THIS VERSION, CHILLI IS ADDED TO THE "HOLY TRINITY" OF ONION, CELERY AND SWEET PEPPER.

SERVES SIX

INGREDIENTS
  450g/1lb fresh mussels
  450g/1lb raw prawns (shrimp),
    in the shell
  1 cooked crab, about 1kg/2¼lb
  small bunch of parsley, leaves
    chopped and stalks reserved
  150ml/¼ pint/⅔ cup vegetable oil
  115g/4oz/1 cup plain
    (all-purpose) flour
  1 green (bell) pepper, seeded
    and chopped
  1 large onion, chopped
  2 celery sticks, sliced
  1 fresh green chilli, seeded
    and chopped
  3 garlic cloves, finely chopped
  75g/3oz smoked spiced sausage,
    skinned and sliced
  275g/10oz/1½ cups white long
    grain rice
  6 spring onions (scallions), sliced
  Tabasco sauce, to taste
  salt

1 Wash the mussels in several changes of cold water, pulling away the black "beards". Discard broken mussels or any that do not close when tapped firmly.

2 Bring 250ml/8fl oz/1 cup water to the boil in a deep pan. Add the prepared mussels, cover the pan tightly and cook over a high heat, shaking frequently, for 3 minutes. As the mussels open, lift them out with tongs into a sieve set over a bowl. Discard any that fail to open. Shell the mussels, discarding most of the shells but reserving a few.

3 Peel the prawns and set them aside, reserving a few for the garnish. Put the shells and heads into the pan.

4 Remove all the meat from the crab, separating the brown and white meat. Add all the pieces of shell to the pan and stir in 5ml/1 tsp salt.

5 Return the mussel liquid from the bowl to the pan and make it up to 2 litres/ 3½ pints/8 cups with water. Bring the shellfish stock to the boil, skimming it regularly. When there is no more froth on the surface, add the parsley stalks and simmer for 15 minutes. Cool the reduced stock, then strain into a liquid measure and make it up to 2 litres/ 3½ pints/8 cups with water.

6 Heat the oil in a heavy pan and stir in the flour. Stir constantly over a medium heat with a wooden spoon or whisk until the roux reaches a golden-brown colour. Immediately add the pepper, onion, celery, chilli and garlic. Continue cooking for about 3 minutes until the onion is soft. Stir in the sausage. Reheat the stock.

7 Stir the brown crab meat into the roux, then ladle in the hot stock a little at a time, stirring constantly until it has all been smoothly incorporated. Bring to a low boil, partially cover the pan, then simmer for 30 minutes.

8 Meanwhile, cook the rice in plenty of lightly salted boiling water until the grains are tender.

9 Add the prawns, mussels, white crab meat and spring onions to the gumbo. Return to the boil and season with salt if necessary. Taste and add a dash or two of Tabasco sauce to heighten the heat generated by the chilli. Simmer for a further minute, then add the chopped parsley leaves. Serve immediately, ladling the soup over the hot rice in soup plates.

COOK'S TIP
It is vital to stir constantly to darken the roux without burning. Should black specks occur at any stage of cooking, discard the roux and start again. Have the pepper, onion, celery, chilli and garlic ready to add to the roux the minute it reaches the correct golden-brown stage, as this stops it from becoming too dark.

CANTONESE FRIED PRAWNS

THIS SPICY DISH FLAVOURED WITH CHILLIES, GINGER AND FRIED SALT AND PEPPERCORNS MAKES A DELICIOUS SUPPERTIME TREAT. SERVE WITH WARM CRUSTY BREAD.

2 Carefully remove and discard the heads and legs from the raw prawns. Leave the body shells and the tails in place. Pat the prepared prawns dry with kitchen paper.

3 Heat the oil for deep-frying to 190°C/375°F or until a cube of day-old bread, added to the oil, browns in 30–45 seconds. Fry the prawns for 1 minute, then lift them out and drain thoroughly on kitchen paper. Spoon 30ml/2 tbsp of the hot oil into a large frying pan, leaving the rest of the oil to one side to cool.

4 Heat the oil in the frying pan. Add the fried salt, with the finely chopped onion, garlic, ginger, chillies and sugar. Toss together for 1 minute, then add the prawns and toss them over the heat for 1 minute more until they are coated and the shells are impregnated with the seasonings. Serve at once, garnished with the spring onions.

SERVES THREE TO FOUR

INGREDIENTS
  15–18 large raw prawns (shrimp),
    in the shell, about 450g/1lb
  vegetable oil, for deep-frying
  1 small onion, finely chopped
  2 garlic cloves, crushed
  1cm/½in piece fresh root ginger,
    peeled and very finely grated
  1–2 fresh red chillies, seeded and
    finely sliced
  2.5ml/½ tsp granulated sugar
  3–4 spring onions (scallions), sliced,
    to garnish
For the fried salt
  10ml/2 tsp salt
  5ml/1 tsp Sichuan peppercorns

1 Make the fried salt by dry-frying the salt and peppercorns in a heavy frying pan over a medium heat until the peppercorns begin to release their aroma. Cool the mixture, then tip into a mortar and crush with a pestle or process in a blender.

COOK'S TIPS
• These succulent prawns beg to be eaten with the fingers, so provide finger bowls or hot cloths for your guests.
• "Fried salt" is also known as "Cantonese salt" or simply "salt and pepper mix". It is widely used as a table condiment or as a dip for deep-fried or roasted food, but can also be an ingredient, as here. It is best when freshly prepared.
• Black or white peppercorns can be substituted for the Sichuan peppercorns.

FISH AND SHELLFISH LAKSA

A LAKSA IS A SOUPY MALAYSIAN STEW OF FISH, POULTRY, MEAT OR VEGETABLES WITH NOODLES.
THIS TYPE OF DISH IS OFTEN VERY HOT AND IS COOLED BY ADDING COCONUT MILK.

SERVES FOUR TO FIVE

INGREDIENTS

   3 fresh medium-hot red chillies,
     seeded and roughly chopped
   4–5 garlic cloves
   5ml/1 tsp mild paprika
   10ml/2 tsp shrimp paste
   25ml/1½ tbsp chopped fresh
     root ginger
   7 small red shallots
   25g/1oz fresh coriander (cilantro),
     preferably with roots
   45ml/3 tbsp groundnut (peanut) oil
   5ml/1 tsp fennel seeds, crushed
   2 fennel bulbs, cut into thin wedges
   600ml/1 pint/2½ cups fish stock
   300g/11oz thin vermicelli
     rice noodles
   450ml/¾ pint/scant 2 cups
     coconut milk
   juice of 1–2 limes
   30–45ml/2–3 tbsp Thai fish sauce
     (*nam pla*)
   450g/1lb firm white fish fillet, cut
     into chunks
   20 large raw prawns (jumbo shrimp),
     peeled and deveined
   small bunch of fresh holy basil or
     regular basil
   2 spring onions (scallions), sliced

1 Process the chillies, garlic, paprika, shrimp paste, ginger and two of the shallots to a paste in a food processor, blender or spice grinder. Remove the roots and stems from the coriander, wash thoroughly and pat dry with kitchen paper. Add them to the paste; chop and reserve the coriander leaves. Add 15ml/1 tbsp of the oil to the paste and process again until fairly smooth. Scrape into a bowl.

2 Heat the remaining oil in a large pan. Add the remaining shallots, with the fennel seeds and fennel wedges. Cook until lightly browned, then add 45ml/ 3 tbsp of the paste and stir-fry for 1–2 minutes. Pour in the fish stock and bring to the boil. Reduce the heat and simmer for 8–10 minutes.

3 Meanwhile, cook the vermicelli rice noodles according to the instructions on the packet. Drain thoroughly and set aside.

4 Pour the coconut milk into the pan of shallots, stirring constantly to prevent sticking, then add the juice of 1 lime, with 30ml/2 tbsp of the fish sauce. Stir well to combine. Bring to a gentle simmer and taste, adding more of the coconut paste, lime juice or fish sauce as necessary.

5 Add the fish to the pan. Cook for 2–3 minutes, then add the raw prawns and cook for a further 3–4 minutes or until they just turn pink.

6 Chop most of the basil and add it to the pan with the reserved chopped coriander leaves.

7 Divide the noodles among 4–5 deep bowls, then ladle in the stew. Sprinkle with spring onions and the remaining whole basil leaves. Serve immediately.

Chillies crop up across the globe, featuring in delectable dishes from places as far apart as Italy and Thailand. This chapter chooses some of the best, from a classic Thai curry to a sweet and spicy Moroccan tagine. From Mexico there's a Spicy Beef Tortilla, and Chilli Beef with Spicy Onion Rings, while Indonesia's choice is Spicy Meatballs, served with a fiery sambal. The collection includes dishes that would do you proud at dinner parties, but also features family favourites such as Penne with Tomato and Chilli Sauce, Hot Pepperoni and Chilli Pizza, and Lamb Stew with Chilli Sauce.

Poultry and Meat Dishes

STIR-FRIED CHICKEN WITH CHILLI AND BASIL

THIS QUICK AND EASY CHICKEN DISH IS AN EXCELLENT INTRODUCTION TO THAI CUISINE. FIERY CHILLIES PARTNER THE HOLY BASIL, WHICH HAS A PUNGENT FLAVOUR THAT IS SPICY AND SHARP.

2 Add the pieces of chicken to the wok and stir-fry until they change colour. Stir in the fish sauce, soy sauce and sugar. Stir-fry the mixture for 3–4 minutes or until the chicken is fully cooked.

3 Stir in the fresh basil leaves. Spoon the mixture on to a warm serving platter, or individual serving dishes, garnish with the chopped chillies and deep-fried basil, and serve.

SERVES FOUR TO SIX

INGREDIENTS
  450g/1lb skinless, boneless
    chicken breast portions
  45ml/3 tbsp vegetable oil
  4 garlic cloves, thinly sliced
  2–4 fresh red chillies, seeded and
    finely chopped
  45ml/3 tbsp Thai fish sauce
    (*nam pla*)
  10ml/2 tsp dark soy sauce
  5ml/1 tsp granulated sugar
  10–12 holy basil leaves
  2 fresh red chillies, seeded and
    finely chopped, to garnish
  about 20 deep-fried holy basil leaves,
    to garnish

1 Using a sharp knife, cut the chicken breasts into bitesize pieces. Heat the oil in a wok. Add the garlic and chillies and stir-fry over a medium heat for 1–2 minutes until the garlic is golden. Do not let the garlic burn or it will taste bitter.

COOK'S TIPS
• Holy basil is native to Asia and it differs from other basils in that heat develops the flavour. The leaves have the typical basil fragrance with the addition of pepper and mint. A substitute is a mix of ordinary basil and spearmint.
• To deep-fry holy basil leaves, first make sure that the leaves are completely dry or they will splutter when added to the oil. Deep-fry the leaves briefly in hot oil until they are crisp and translucent – this will only take about 30–40 seconds. Lift out the leaves using a slotted spoon or wire basket and leave them to drain on kitchen paper.

THAI FRIED RICE <u>WITH</u> CHICKEN <u>AND</u> CHILLIES

THIS SUBSTANTIAL DISH IS BASED ON THAI FRAGRANT RICE, WHICH IS SOMETIMES KNOWN AS JASMINE RICE. CHICKEN, RED PEPPER AND CHILLIES ADD COLOUR AND EXTRA FLAVOUR.

SERVES FOUR

INGREDIENTS
475ml/16fl oz/2 cups water
50g/2oz/½ cup coconut milk powder
350g/12oz/1¾ cups Thai fragrant
    rice, rinsed and well drained
30ml/2 tbsp groundnut (peanut) oil
2 garlic cloves, chopped
1 small onion, finely chopped
2.5cm/1in piece fresh root
    ginger, grated
225g/8oz skinless, boneless chicken
    breast portions, cut into
    1cm/½in dice
1 red (bell) pepper, seeded
    and sliced
1 fresh red chilli, seeded
    and chopped
115g/4oz/⅔ cup drained canned
    sweetcorn kernels
5ml/1 tsp chilli oil
5ml/1 tsp curry powder
2 eggs, beaten
salt
spring onion (scallion) shreds,
    to garnish

2 Heat the oil in a wok, add the garlic, onion and ginger, and stir-fry over a medium heat for 2 minutes.

3 Push the vegetables to the sides of the wok, add the chicken to the centre and stir-fry for 2 minutes. Add the rice. Stir-fry over a high heat for 3 minutes.

4 Stir in the sliced red pepper, chilli, sweetcorn, chilli oil and curry powder, with salt to taste. Toss over the heat for 1 minute. Stir in the beaten eggs and cook for 1 minute more. Everything should be piping hot before serving. Transfer to a heated serving dish, garnish with spring onion shreds and serve.

1 Pour the water into a pan and whisk in the coconut milk powder. Add the rice and bring to the boil. Reduce the heat, cover and cook for 12 minutes or until the rice is tender and the liquid has been absorbed. Remove from the heat at once and spread the rice on a baking sheet and leave until cold.

COOK'S TIP
It is important that the rice is completely cold before being fried. The oil should be very hot when the rice is added.

RED CHICKEN CURRY <u>WITH</u> BAMBOO SHOOTS

THE CHILLI PASTE THAT IS THE BASIS OF THIS DISH HAS A SUPERB FLAVOUR AND WILL COME IN USEFUL IN ALL SORTS OF SPICY DISHES, SO IT IS WORTH MAKING IT IN QUANTITY.

SERVES FOUR TO SIX

INGREDIENTS
    1 litre/1¾ pints/4 cups coconut milk
    450g/1lb skinless, boneless chicken
      breast portions, diced
    30ml/2 tbsp Thai fish sauce (*nam pla*)
    15ml/1 tbsp granulated sugar
    225g/8oz canned bamboo shoots,
      rinsed and sliced
    5 kaffir lime leaves, torn
    salt and ground black pepper
For the red curry paste
    12–15 fresh red chillies, seeded
    4 shallots, thinly sliced
    2 garlic cloves, chopped
    15ml/1 tbsp chopped fresh galangal
    2 lemon grass stalks, tender
      portions chopped
    3 kaffir lime leaves, chopped
    4 coriander (cilantro) roots
    10 black peppercorns
    5ml/1 tsp coriander seeds
    2.5ml/½ tsp cumin seeds
    good pinch of ground cinnamon
    5ml/1 tsp ground turmeric
    2.5ml/½ tsp shrimp paste
    30ml/2 tbsp oil
To garnish
    2 fresh red chillies, chopped
    10–12 fresh basil leaves
    10–12 fresh mint leaves

1 Make the red curry paste. Combine all the ingredients except for the oil in a mortar. Add 5ml/1 tsp salt. Pound with a pestle, or process in a food processor, until smooth. If you are using a pestle and mortar, you might need to pound the ingredients in batches and then combine them.

2 Add the oil to the paste a little at a time and blend in well. If you are using a food processor or blender, add it slowly through the feeder tube. Scrape the paste into a jar and store in the refrigerator until ready to use.

3 Pour half the coconut milk into a large heavy pan. Gently bring to the boil, stirring all the time until the milk separates, then reduce the heat.

4 Add 30ml/2 tbsp of the red curry paste, stir to mix, and cook for a few minutes to allow the flavours to develop. The sauce should begin to thicken and may need to be stirred frequently to prevent it from sticking to the pan. Add a little more coconut milk if necessary.

5 Add the chicken, fish sauce and sugar. Fry for 3–5 minutes until the chicken changes colour, stirring constantly to prevent it from sticking.

6 Add the rest of the coconut milk, with the bamboo shoots and kaffir lime leaves. Bring back to the boil. Stir in salt and pepper to taste. Serve garnished with the chillies, basil and mint leaves.

COOK'S TIPS
• The surplus curry paste can be stored in a sealed jar in the refrigerator for 3–4 weeks. Alternatively, freeze it in small tubs, each containing about 30ml/2 tbsp.
• Young bamboo shoots are cultivated in China for the table. The preparation is laborious, so the canned shoots are used in the West. They provide a crunchy texture, and are a useful contrast to other ingredients.
• The roots of coriander have a deep earthy fragrance and are used widely in Thai cooking. They can be frozen for storage until you need them. Simply cut the roots off and wrap in clear film (plastic wrap).

CHICKEN WITH CHIPOTLE SAUCE

THIS IS A VERY EASY RECIPE FOR ENTERTAINING, WITH JUST A FEW KEY INGREDIENTS, INCLUDING DRIED CHILLIES. IT IS COOKED IN THE OVEN AND NEEDS NO LAST-MINUTE ATTENTION.

SERVES SIX

INGREDIENTS
  6 chipotle chillies
  chicken stock (see method
    for quantity)
  3 onions
  45ml/3 tbsp vegetable oil
  6 skinless, boneless chicken
    breast portions
  salt and ground black pepper
  fresh oregano, to garnish
  boiled rice, to serve

3 Peel the onions. Using a sharp knife, cut them in half, then slice them thinly. Separate the slices.

6 Arrange the chicken on top of the onion slices. Sprinkle with a little salt and several grindings of pepper.

1 Put the dried chillies in a bowl and pour over hot water to cover. Leave to stand for at least 20 minutes, until very soft. Drain, reserving the soaking water in a liquid measure. Cut off the stalk from each chilli, then slit them lengthways and scrape out the seeds with a small sharp knife.

4 Heat the oil in a large frying pan, add the onions and cook over a low to moderate heat for about 5 minutes, or until they have softened but not coloured, stirring occasionally.

5 Using a slotted spoon, transfer the onion slices to a casserole that is large enough to hold all the chicken breast portions in a single layer. Sprinkle the onion slices with a little salt and ground black pepper.

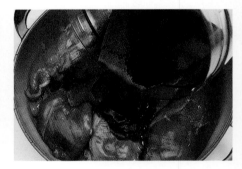

7 Pour the chipotle purée over the chicken, making sure that each piece is evenly coated.

8 Bake in the oven for 45–60 minutes or until the chicken is cooked through, but is still moist and tender. Garnish with fresh oregano and serve with boiled white rice.

2 Preheat the oven to 180°C/350°F/ Gas 4. Chop the flesh of the chillies roughly and put it in a food processor or blender. Add enough chicken stock to the soaking water to make it up to 400ml/14fl oz/1⅔ cups. Pour it into the processor and process until smooth.

COOK'S TIPS
• It is important to seek out chipotle chillies, as they impart a wonderfully rich and smoky flavour to the chicken.
• Dried chillies of various types can be bought by mail order, as well as from specialist food stores.
• The chilli purée can be prepared ahead of time.
• If tears come to your eyes when peeling onions, peel them under water. Then pat dry with kitchen paper before slicing.

VARIATION
Prepare the chipotles as in the main method. Put them in a stainless steel pan along with the soaking water; 2 peeled tomatoes, cut in wedges; ½ a sweet onion, chopped; 4 garlic cloves and 75ml/5 tbsp chopped fresh coriander (cilantro). Add water if needed to just cover. Simmer for 30 minutes. Dry-fry 15ml/1 tbsp cumin seeds, grind in a mortar or process in a blender and add to the chilli mixture. Cook for 5 minutes, season with salt, and purée. It will keep for 1 week in the refrigerator.

HOT PEPPERONI AND CHILLI PIZZA

THERE ARE FEW TREATS MORE TASTY THAN A HOME-MADE FRESHLY BAKED PIZZA.

SERVES FOUR

INGREDIENTS
225g/8oz/2 cups strong white
  (bread) flour
10ml/2 tsp easy-blend (rapid-rise)
  dried yeast
5ml/1 tsp granulated sugar
2.5ml/½ tsp salt
15ml/1 tbsp olive oil
175ml/6fl oz/¾ cup mixed hand-hot
  milk and water
fresh oregano leaves, to garnish
For the topping
400g/14oz can chopped tomatoes,
  well drained
2 garlic cloves, crushed
5ml/1 tsp dried oregano
225g/8oz mozzarella cheese,
  coarsely grated
2 dried red chillies
225g/8oz pepperoni, sliced
30ml/2 tbsp drained capers

1 Sift the flour into a bowl. Stir in the yeast, sugar and salt. Make a well in the centre. Stir the olive oil into the milk and water, then stir the mixture into the flour. Mix to a soft dough.

2 Knead the dough on a lightly floured surface for 5–10 minutes until it is smooth and elastic. Return it to the clean, lightly oiled, bowl and cover with clear film (plastic wrap). Leave in a warm place for about 30 minutes or until the dough has doubled in bulk.

3 Preheat the oven to 220°C/425°F/Gas 7. Knead the dough on a lightly floured surface for 1 minute. Divide it in half and roll each piece out to a 25cm/10in circle. Place on lightly oiled pizza trays or baking sheets.

4 Make the topping. Tip the drained tomatoes into a bowl and stir in the crushed garlic and dried oregano.

5 Spread half the mixture over each round, leaving a clear margin around the edge. Set half the mozzarella aside. Divide the rest between the pizzas. Bake for 7–10 minutes until the dough rim on each pizza is pale golden.

6 Crumble the chillies over the pizzas, then arrange the pepperoni slices and capers on top. Sprinkle with the reserved mozzarella. Return the pizzas to the oven and bake for 7–10 minutes more. Sprinkle over the fresh oregano and serve immediately.

VARIATION
Use bacon instead of sliced pepperoni. Grill (broil) about 6 slices and crumble them over the pizza with the chillies. Omit the capers.

PENNE <u>WITH</u> TOMATO <u>AND</u> CHILLI SAUCE

IN ITS NATIVE ITALY, THIS PASTA DISH GOES UNDER THE NAME "PENNE ALL'ARRABBIATA".

3 Add the chopped mushrooms to the pan and cook in the same way. Remove and set aside with the pancetta or bacon. Crumble 1 dried chilli into the pan, add the garlic and cook gently, stirring, for a few minutes until the garlic turns golden.

4 Add the tomatoes and basil and season with salt. Cook gently, stirring occasionally, for 10–15 minutes. Meanwhile, bring a large pan of salted water to the boil and cook the penne, following the instructions on the packet.

5 Add the pancetta or bacon and the mushrooms to the tomato sauce. Taste for seasoning, adding another chilli if you prefer a hotter flavour. If the sauce is too dry, stir in a tablespoon or so of the pasta water.

6 Drain the pasta and tip it into a warmed bowl. Dice the remaining butter, add it to the pasta with the cheeses, then toss until well coated. Pour the tomato sauce over the pasta, toss well and serve immediately on warmed plates, with a few basil leaves sprinkled on top.

SERVES FOUR

INGREDIENTS
    25g/1oz/½ cup dried
      porcini mushrooms
    90g/3½oz/7 tbsp butter
    150g/5oz pancetta or rindless
      smoked streaky (fatty) bacon, diced
    1–2 dried red chillies
    2 garlic cloves, crushed
    8 ripe Italian plum tomatoes, peeled
      and chopped
    a few fresh basil leaves, torn, plus
      extra to garnish
    350g/12oz/3 cups fresh or
      dried penne
    50g/2oz/⅔ cup freshly grated
      Parmesan cheese
    25g/1oz/⅓ cup freshly grated
      Pecorino cheese
    salt

1 Soak the dried mushrooms in warm water to cover for 15–20 minutes. Drain, squeeze dry with your hands, then chop finely.

2 Melt 50g/2oz/4 tbsp of the butter in a medium pan. Add the pancetta or bacon and stir-fry until golden and slightly crisp. Remove the pancetta with a slotted spoon and set it aside.

PORK-STUFFED CHILLIES <u>IN</u> WALNUT SAUCE

THE POTATO AND MEAT FILLING IN THESE CHILLIES IS A GOOD PARTNER FOR THE RICH, CREAMY SAUCE THAT COVERS THEM. A GREEN SALAD GOES WELL WITH THIS DISH.

SERVES FOUR

INGREDIENTS
  8 ancho chillies
  1 large waxy potato, about 200g/7oz
  45ml/3 tbsp vegetable oil
  115g/4oz lean minced (ground) pork
  50g/2oz/½ cup plain
    (all-purpose) flour
  2.5ml/½ tsp ground white pepper
  2 eggs, separated
  oil, for deep-frying
  salt
  chopped fresh herbs, to garnish
For the sauce
  1 onion, chopped
  5ml/1 tsp ground cinnamon
  115g/4oz/1 cup walnuts or pecan
    nuts, roughly chopped
  50g/2oz/½ cup chopped almonds
  150g/5oz/⅔ cup cream cheese
  50g/2oz/½ cup soft goat's cheese
  120ml/4fl oz/½ cup single
    (light) cream
  120ml/4fl oz/½ cup dry sherry

1 Soak the dried chillies in a bowl of hot water for 20–30 minutes until softened. Drain, then slit them down one side. Scrape out the seeds, taking care to keep the chillies intact.

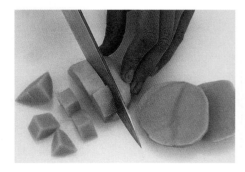

2 Peel the potato and cut it into 1cm/½in cubes. Heat 15ml/1 tbsp of the oil in a large frying pan, add the pork and cook, stirring, until it has browned evenly.

COOK'S TIP
The potatoes must not break or become too floury. Do not overcook.

3 Add the potato cubes and mix well. Cover and cook over a low heat for 25–30 minutes, stirring occasionally. Season with salt, then remove the filling from the heat and set it aside.

4 Make the sauce. Heat the remaining oil in a separate pan and fry the onion with the cinnamon for 3–4 minutes or until softened. Stir in the nuts and fry for 3–4 minutes more.

5 Add both types of cheese to the pan, with the single cream and dry sherry. Mix well for the flavours to blend. Reduce the heat to the lowest setting and cook until the cheese melts and the sauce starts to thicken. Taste the sauce and season it if necessary.

6 Spread out the flour on a plate or in a shallow dish. Season with the white pepper. Beat the egg yolks in a bowl until they are pale and thick.

7 In a separate, grease-free bowl, whisk the whites until they form soft peaks. Add a generous pinch of salt, then fold in the yolks, a little at a time.

8 Spoon some of the filling into each chilli. Pat the outside dry with kitchen paper. Heat the oil for deep-frying to a temperature of 180°C/350°F.

9 Coat a chilli in flour, then dip it in the egg batter, covering it completely. Drain for a few seconds, then add to the hot oil. Add several more battered chillies, but do not overcrowd the pan. Fry the chillies until golden, then lift out and drain on kitchen paper. Keep hot while cooking successive batches.

10 Reheat the walnut and cheese sauce over a low heat, if necessary. Arrange the chillies on individual plates, spoon a little sauce over each and serve immediately, sprinkled with chopped fresh herbs.

LAMB TAGINE WITH SWEET POTATOES

THIS WARMING DISH IS EATEN DURING THE WINTER IN MOROCCO WHERE, ESPECIALLY IN THE MOUNTAINS, THE WEATHER CAN BE SURPRISINGLY COLD.

SERVES FOUR

INGREDIENTS

   900g/2lb braising or
     stewing lamb
   30ml/2 tbsp sunflower oil
   good pinch of ground turmeric
   1 large onion, chopped
   1 fresh red or green chilli, seeded
     and chopped
   7.5ml/1½ tsp paprika
   good pinch of cayenne pepper
   2.5ml/½ tsp ground cumin
   450g/1lb sweet potatoes
   15ml/1 tbsp chopped fresh parsley,
     plus extra to garnish
   15ml/1 tbsp chopped fresh
     coriander (cilantro)
   15g/½oz/1 tbsp butter
   salt and ground black pepper

1 Trim the meat and cut into cubes. Heat the oil in a flameproof casserole and add the meat. Sprinkle with the turmeric and fry for 3–4 minutes until evenly brown, stirring frequently. Cover the pan tightly and cook for 15 minutes over a fairly gentle heat, without lifting the lid. Preheat the oven to 180°C/350°F/Gas 4.

2 Add the onion, chilli, paprika, cayenne pepper and cumin to the casserole and season. Pour in enough water to cover the meat. Cover tightly and cook in the oven for 1–1½ hours until the meat is very tender, checking occasionally and adding a little extra water to keep the stew fairly moist.

3 Meanwhile, peel the sweet potatoes and slice them straight into a pan of salted water (sweet potatoes discolour very quickly if exposed to the air). Bring to the boil, then simmer for 2–3 minutes until just tender. Drain.

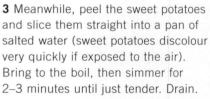

4 Stir the herbs into the meat, adding a little extra water if the stew appears dry. Arrange the sweet potato slices over the meat and dot with the butter. Cover and cook in the oven, covered, for a further 10 minutes or until the potatoes feel very tender when tested with a skewer. Increase the oven temperature to 200°C/400°F/Gas 6.

5 Remove the lid of the casserole and cook in the oven for a further 10 minutes until the potatoes are golden. Garnish and serve immediately.

LAMB STEW WITH CHILLI SAUCE

THE DRIED CHILLIES IN THIS STEW ADD DEPTH AND RICHNESS TO THE SAUCE, WHILE THE POTATO SLICES ENSURE THAT IT IS SUBSTANTIAL ENOUGH TO SERVE ON ITS OWN.

SERVES SIX

INGREDIENTS

6 guajillo chillies, seeded
2 pasilla chillies, seeded
250ml/8fl oz/1 cup hot water
3 garlic cloves, peeled
5ml/1 tsp ground cinnamon
2.5ml/½ tsp ground cloves
2.5ml/½ tsp ground black pepper
15ml/1 tbsp vegetable oil
1kg/2¼lb lean boneless lamb
  shoulder, cut into 2cm/¾in cubes
2 large potatoes, scrubbed and cut
  into 1cm/½in thick slices
salt
strips of red (bell) pepper and fresh
  oregano, to garnish

COOK'S TIP
When frying the lamb, don't be tempted to cook too many cubes at one time, or the meat will steam rather than fry.

1 Snap or tear the dried chillies into large pieces, put them in a bowl and pour over the hot water. Leave to soak for 20–30 minutes, then tip the contents of the bowl into a food processor or blender. Add the garlic and spices. Process until smooth.

2 Heat the oil in a large pan. Add the lamb cubes, in batches, and stir-fry over a high heat until the cubes are browned on all sides.

3 Return all the lamb cubes to the pan, spread them out, then cover them with a layer of potato slices. Add salt to taste. Put a lid on the pan and cook over a medium heat for 10 minutes.

4 Pour over the chilli mixture and mix well. Replace the lid and simmer over a low heat for about 1 hour or until the meat and the potato are tender. Serve with a rice dish, and garnish with strips of red pepper and fresh oregano.

SPICY MEATBALLS

THESE SPICY LITTLE PATTIES COME FROM INDONESIA. SERVE THEM WITH BROAD EGG NOODLES AND FIERY CHILLI SAMBAL AS A DIPPING SAUCE.

SERVES FOUR TO SIX

INGREDIENTS
 1cm/½in cube shrimp paste
 1 large onion, roughly chopped
 1–2 fresh red chillies, seeded
  and chopped
 2 garlic cloves, crushed
 15ml/1 tbsp coriander seeds
 5ml/1 tsp cumin seeds
 450g/1lb lean minced (ground) beef
 10ml/2 tsp dark soy sauce
 5ml/1 tsp soft dark brown sugar
 juice of 1½ lemons
 a little beaten egg
 vegetable oil, for shallow frying
 salt and ground black pepper
 1 fresh green and 1–2 fresh red
  chillies, to garnish
 Chilli Sambal (below), to serve

1 Wrap the shrimp paste in a piece of foil and gently warm it in a dry frying pan for 5 minutes, turning a few times. Unwrap the paste and put in a food processor or blender.

COOK'S TIP
When processing the shrimp paste, onion, chillies and garlic, do not run the machine for too long, or the onion will become too wet and spoil the consistency of the meatballs.

2 Add the onion, chillies and garlic to the food processor and process until finely chopped. Set aside. Dry-fry the coriander and cumin seeds in a hot frying pan for 1 minute, to release the aroma. Tip the seeds into a mortar and grind with a pestle.

3 Put the meat in a large bowl. Stir in the onion mixture. Add the ground spices, soy sauce, brown sugar, lemon juice and beaten egg. Season to taste.

4 Shape the meat mixture into small, even-size balls, and chill these for 5–10 minutes to firm them up.

5 Heat the oil in a wok or large frying pan and fry the meatballs for 4–5 minutes, turning often, until cooked through and browned. You may have to do this in batches.

6 Drain the meatballs on kitchen paper, and then pile them on to a warm serving platter or into a large serving bowl. Finely slice the green chilli and one of the red chillies, and sprinkle over the meatballs. Garnish with a whole red chilli, if you like. Serve with the sambal, spooned into a small dish.

VARIATIONS
Beef is traditionally used for this dish, but pork, lamb – or even turkey – would also be good.

CHILLI SAMBAL

THIS FIERCE CONDIMENT IS BOTTLED AS SAMBAL OELEK, BUT IT IS EASY TO PREPARE AND WILL KEEP FOR SEVERAL WEEKS IN A WELL-SEALED JAR IN THE REFRIGERATOR.

MAKES 450G/1LB

INGREDIENTS
 450g/1lb fresh red chillies, seeded
 10ml/2 tsp salt

COOK'S TIP
If any sambal drips on your fingers, wash well in soapy water *immediately.*

1 Bring a pan of water to the boil, add the seeded chillies and cook them for 5–8 minutes.

2 Drain the chillies and chop roughly. Grind the chillies in a food processor or blender, without making the paste too smooth. If you like, you can do this in batches.

3 Scrape into a screw-topped glass jar, stir in the salt and cover with a piece of greaseproof (waxed) paper or clear film (plastic wrap). Screw on the lid and store in the refrigerator. Wash all implements in soapy water. Spoon into dishes using a stainless-steel or plastic spoon. Serve as an accompaniment, as suggested in recipes.

CHILLI BEEF WITH SPICY ONION RINGS

FRUITY, SMOKY AND MILD MEXICAN CHILLIES COMBINE WELL WITH GARLIC IN THIS MARINADE FOR BEEF. ONCE YOU HAVE TASTED THE SPICY ONION RINGS, YOU WILL FIND THEM HARD TO RESIST.

SERVES FOUR

INGREDIENTS
   4 rump (round) or rib-eye beef
     steaks, about 225g/8oz each
For the chilli paste
   3 large pasilla chillies
   2 garlic cloves, finely chopped
   5ml/1 tsp ground toasted
     cumin seeds
   5ml/1 tsp dried oregano
   60ml/4 tbsp olive oil
   salt and ground black pepper
For the spicy onion rings
   2 onions, sliced and separated
     into rings
   250ml/8fl oz/1 cup milk
   75g/3oz/½ cup coarse corn
     meal polenta
   2.5ml/½ tsp dried red chilli flakes
   5ml/1 tsp ground toasted
     cumin seeds
   5ml/1 tsp dried oregano
   vegetable oil, for deep-frying

1 To make the chilli paste, cut the stalks from the chillies, then slit them and shake out most of the seeds. Toast the chillies in a dry frying pan for 2–4 minutes, until they give off their aroma. Place the chillies in a bowl, cover with warm water and leave to soak for 20–30 minutes.

2 Drain the chillies, reserving the soaking water. Put them in a food processor or blender. Add the garlic, cumin, oregano and oil. Process to a smooth paste, adding a little soaking water, if necessary. It should not be too stiff. Season with pepper.

3 Pour the chilli paste all over the meat. Put the steaks in a dish, cover and leave to marinate in the refrigerator for up to 12 hours.

COOK'S TIP
It is always best to allow a few minutes resting time for the steaks after cooking. It relaxes the meat, making it more tender.

4 Make the onion rings. Soak the onions in the milk for 30 minutes. Mix the corn meal, chilli, cumin and oregano in a shallow bowl and season with salt and pepper. Heat the oil for deep-frying to 160–180°C/325–350°F or until a cube of day-old bread browns in about 45 seconds. Drain the onion rings and dip into the corn meal mixture. Fry in batches for 2–4 minutes, until browned and crisp. Do not overcrowd the pan. Drain on kitchen paper.

5 Prepare the barbecue or heat a cast-iron griddle pan. Season the steaks with salt and cook for about 5 minutes on each side for a medium result; adjust the timing for rare or well-done steak. Serve the steaks while hot with the onion rings.

MEXICAN SPICY BEEF TORTILLA

THIS DISH IS NOT UNLIKE A LASAGNE, EXCEPT THAT THE SPICY MEAT IS MIXED WITH RICE AND IS LAYERED BETWEEN MEXICAN TORTILLAS, WITH A HOT SALSA SAUCE FOR AN EXTRA KICK.

SERVES FOUR

INGREDIENTS

1 onion, chopped
2 garlic cloves, crushed
1 fresh red chilli, seeded and sliced
350g/12oz rump (round) steak, cut
    into small cubes
15ml/1 tbsp oil
225g/8oz/2 cups cooked long
    grain rice
beef stock, to moisten
salt and ground black pepper
3 large wheat tortillas
For the salsa picante
2 × 400g/14oz cans
    chopped tomatoes
2 garlic cloves, halved
1 onion, quartered
1–2 fresh red chillies, seeded and
    roughly chopped
5ml/1 tsp ground cumin
2.5–5ml/½–1 tsp cayenne pepper
5ml/1 tsp chopped fresh oregano
tomato juice or water, if required
For the cheese sauce
50g/2oz/¼ cup butter
50g/2oz/½ cup plain
    (all-purpose) flour
600ml/1 pint/2½ cups milk
115g/4oz/1 cup grated
    Cheddar cheese

1 Make the salsa picante. Place the first 4 ingredients in a blender or food processor and process until smooth.

2 Pour into a pan, add the spices and oregano, and season with salt. Bring to the boil, stirring occasionally. Boil for 1–2 minutes, then lower the heat, cover and simmer for 15 minutes. The sauce should be thick, but of a pouring consistency. If it is too thick, dilute it with a little tomato juice or water. Preheat the oven to 180°C/350°F/Gas 4.

COOK'S TIP
You can use any type of beef for this dish. If stewing steak is used, it should be very finely chopped and the cooking time increased by 10–15 minutes.

3 Make the cheese sauce. Melt the butter in a pan and stir in the flour. Cook for 1 minute. Add the milk, stirring all the time until the sauce boils and thickens. Stir in all but 30ml/2 tbsp of the cheese and season. Set aside.

4 Put the onion, garlic and chilli in a large bowl. Mix in the meat. Heat the oil in a pan and stir-fry the meat for 10 minutes or until it has browned. Stir in the rice and stock to moisten. Season to taste.

5 Pour about one-quarter of the cheese sauce into the base of a round ovenproof dish. Add a tortilla and then spread over half the salsa followed by half the meat mixture.

6 Repeat these layers, then add half the remaining cheese sauce and the final tortilla. Pour over the remaining cheese sauce and sprinkle the reserved cheese on top. Bake in the oven for 15–20 minutes until golden on top.

Get into the habit of buying fresh chillies whenever you
see them on sale, and you'll be surprised how often
you'll use them in cooking, not necessarily as the
principal ingredient, but for pungent punctuation.
Chillies are great for highlighting other flavours, and
nowhere is this more apparent than when they are added
to vegetable and vegetarian dishes. Try Couscous with
Eggs and Spicy Relish, Lentil Dhal with Chillies and
Roasted Garlic, or Chinese Chilli Noodles.

Vegetarian
Main Meals

CHILLI AND PAK CHOI OMELETTE PARCELS

COLOURFUL STIR-FRIED VEGETABLES AND CORIANDER IN BLACK BEAN SAUCE MAKE A REMARKABLY GOOD OMELETTE FILLING, WHICH IS QUICK AND EASY TO PREPARE.

SERVES FOUR

INGREDIENTS
  130g/4½oz broccoli, cut into
    small florets
  30ml/2 tbsp groundnut (peanut) oil
  1cm/½in piece fresh root ginger,
    finely grated
  1 large garlic clove, crushed
  2 fresh red chillies, seeded and
    finely sliced
  4 spring onions (scallions),
    diagonally sliced
  175g/6oz/3 cups pak choi
    (bok choy), shredded
  50g/2oz/2 cups fresh coriander
    (cilantro) leaves, plus extra
    to garnish
  115g/4oz/2 cups beansprouts
  45ml/3 tbsp black bean sauce
  4 eggs
  salt and ground black pepper

1 Bring a pan of lightly salted water to the boil and blanch the broccoli for 2 minutes. Drain, then refresh under cold running water, and drain again.

2 Heat 15ml/1 tbsp of the oil in a frying pan and stir-fry the ginger, garlic and half the chilli for 1 minute. Add the spring onions, broccoli and pak choi, and toss the mixture over the heat for 2 minutes more.

3 Chop three-quarters of the coriander and add to the frying pan. Add the beansprouts and stir-fry for 1 minute, then add the black bean sauce and heat through for 1 minute more. Remove the pan from the heat and keep warm.

4 Mix the eggs lightly with a fork and season well. Heat a little of the remaining oil in a small frying pan and add one-quarter of the beaten egg. Tilt the pan so that the egg covers the base, then sprinkle over one-quarter of the reserved coriander leaves. Cook until set, then turn out the omelette on to a plate and keep warm while you make 3 more omelettes.

5 Spoon one-quarter of the stir-fry on to each omelette and roll up. Cut in half crossways and serve, garnished with coriander leaves and chilli slices.

COOK'S TIP
If you overdo the chilli, don't reach for a glass of water. Drinking it will simply spread the discomfort. Instead, eat something starchy, such as a piece of bread, or try a spoonful of yogurt.

CHINESE CHILLI NOODLES

THERE ARE PLENTY OF CONTRASTING TEXTURES IN THIS SPICY STIR-FRY. CRISP GREEN BEANS AND BEANSPROUTS VERSUS NOODLES AND OMELETTE STRIPS MAKES FOR AN INTERESTING DISH.

SERVES FOUR

INGREDIENTS
2 eggs
5ml/1 tsp chilli powder
5ml/1 tsp ground turmeric
60ml/4 tbsp vegetable oil
1 large onion, finely sliced
2 fresh red chillies, seeded and
  finely sliced
15ml/1 tbsp soy sauce
2 large cooked potatoes, cut into
  small cubes
6 pieces fried beancurd
  (tofu), sliced
225g/8oz/4 cups beansprouts
115g/4oz green beans, blanched
350g/12oz fresh thick
  egg noodles
salt and ground black pepper
sliced spring onions (scallions),
  to garnish

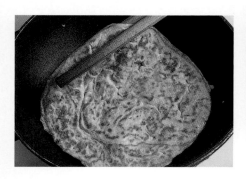

1 Beat the eggs lightly, then strain them through a fine sieve into a bowl. Heat a lightly greased omelette pan. Pour in half of the beaten egg and tilt the pan quickly to cover the base thinly. When the egg is just set, turn the omelette over, using chopsticks or a spatula, and fry the other side.

2 Slide the omelette on to a plate, blot with kitchen paper, roll up and cut into narrow strips. Make a second omelette in the same way and slice. Set the omelette strips aside for the garnish.

3 In a cup, mix together the chilli powder and turmeric. Form a paste by stirring in a little water.

4 Heat the oil in a wok or frying pan. Fry the onion until soft. Reduce the heat and stir in the chilli paste, chillies and soy sauce. Fry for 2 minutes.

5 Add the potatoes and fry for about 2 minutes, mixing well with the chillies. Add the beancurd, the beansprouts, green beans and noodles.

6 Gently stir-fry until the noodles are evenly coated and heated through. Take care not to break up the potatoes or the beancurd. Season with salt and pepper. Serve hot, garnished with the reserved omelette strips and spring onion slices.

COOK'S TIPS
• When making this dish for non-vegetarians, or for vegetarians who eat fish, add a piece of shrimp paste. A small chunk about the size of a stock (bouillon) cube, mashed with the chilli paste, will add a rich, aromatic flavour.
• Most chilli powder we buy is actually a blended mixture of ground dried red chillies, cumin, oregano and salt, often with a little garlic powder mixed in. For a pure powder, you'll need to find a specialist food store or order by mail.

COUSCOUS WITH EGGS AND SPICY RELISH

A RICHLY FLAVOURED ROASTED TOMATO SAUCE, SPIKED WITH CHILLI, IS AN IDEAL TOPPING FOR LIGHTLY COOKED EGGS IN A SAVOURY COUSCOUS NEST.

SERVES FOUR

INGREDIENTS

675g/1½lb plum tomatoes,
  roughly chopped
4 garlic cloves, chopped
75ml/5 tbsp olive oil
½ fresh red chilli, seeded
  and chopped
10ml/2 tsp soft light
  brown sugar
4 eggs
1 large onion, chopped
2 celery sticks, finely sliced
50g/2oz/⅓ cup sultanas
  (golden raisins)
200g/7oz/generous 1 cup ready-to-
  use couscous
about 350ml/12fl oz/1½ cups hot
  vegetable stock
salt and ground black pepper

1 Preheat the oven to 200°C/400°F/ Gas 6. Put the tomatoes and garlic in a roasting pan, drizzle with 30ml/2 tbsp of the oil, sprinkle with chopped chilli, sugar and salt and pepper, and roast for 20 minutes until soft.

VARIATION
Add a drained bottled pimiento or two to the tomato mixture before sieving it.

2 Lower the eggs carefully into boiling water and boil them for 4 minutes, then plunge them straight into cold water. When cold, shell them carefully.

3 Remove the tomatoes from the oven and push them through a sieve. Add 15ml/1 tbsp boiling water and 15ml/ 1 tbsp olive oil to the puréed tomatoes and blend to give a smooth, rich sauce. Season to taste with salt and pepper. Keep the sauce hot while you prepare the couscous.

4 Put 15–30ml/1–2 tbsp of the remaining olive oil in a large pan and gently fry the onion and celery until softened. Add the sultanas, couscous and hot stock, and set aside until all the liquid has been absorbed. This will take about 7 minutes. Stir gently, add extra hot stock if necessary and season to taste.

5 Spread out the couscous on to a large heated serving dish, half bury the eggs in it and spoon a little tomato sauce over the top of each egg. Serve immediately, with the rest of the sauce handed separately.

SPAGHETTI WITH GARLIC, CHILLI AND OIL

PASTA DESCRIBED AS AL DENTE HAS A BIT OF BITE. THERE'S ANOTHER BITE THAT IS IMPORTANT, AND THAT'S ANY INGREDIENT GIVING A BIT OF AN EDGE TO A BLAND DISH. CHILLIES DO THE JOB SUPERBLY.

1 Bring a large pan of salted water to the boil and add the spaghetti, lowering it into the water gradually, as it softens. Cook for 10–12 minutes, or according to the packet instructions, until the strands are *al dente.*

2 Meanwhile, heat the oil very gently in a small pan. Add the crushed garlic and chopped dried chilli and stir over a low heat until the garlic is just beginning to brown. Remove the chilli and discard it.

3 Drain the pasta and tip it into a large heated bowl. Pour on the oil and garlic mixture, add the parsley and toss vigorously until the pasta glistens. Serve immediately, garnished with extra dried chillies.

SERVES FOUR

INGREDIENTS
- 400g/14oz spaghetti
- 90ml/6 tbsp extra virgin olive oil
- 2–4 garlic cloves, crushed
- 1 dried red chilli, chopped, plus extra dried chillies to garnish
- 1 small handful fresh flat leaf parsley, roughly chopped
- salt

COOK'S TIPS
- Use a fresh chilli, if you prefer.
- For extra heat, substitute chilli oil for some or all of the olive oil. Be careful when using chilli oil because the flavour becomes very concentrated, so use it sparingly.
- If you like, hand separately a bowl of freshly grated Parmesan cheese. The delicious flavour of this cheese is better appreciated when fresh. A block will keep well in the refrigerator, wrapped in clear film (plastic wrap).

CHILLI CHEESE TORTILLA <u>WITH</u> FRESH TOMATO <u>AND</u> CORIANDER SALSA

GOOD WARM OR COLD, THIS IS LIKE A SLICED POTATO QUICHE WITHOUT THE PASTRY BASE, AND IS WELL SPIKED WITH CHILLI. IT MAKES A SATISFYING LUNCH.

SERVES FOUR

INGREDIENTS
  45ml/3 tbsp sunflower or
  olive oil
  1 small onion, thinly sliced
  2–3 fresh green jalapeño chillies,
  seeded and sliced
  200g/7oz cold cooked potato,
  thinly sliced
  150g/5oz/1¼ cups grated cheese
  6 eggs, beaten
  salt and ground black pepper
  fresh herbs and chilli, to garnish
For the salsa
  500g/1¼lb flavoursome tomatoes,
  peeled, seeded and finely chopped
  1 fresh mild green chilli, seeded and
  finely chopped
  2 garlic cloves, crushed
  45ml/3 tbsp chopped fresh
  coriander (cilantro)
  juice of 1 lime
  2.5ml/½ tsp salt

1 Make the salsa by mixing all the ingredients in a bowl. Mix well, cover and set aside.

2 Heat 15ml/1 tbsp of the oil in a large frying pan and gently fry the onion and jalapeños for 5 minutes, stirring until softened. Add the potato and cook for 5 minutes until lightly browned, keeping the slices whole. Using a slotted spoon, transfer the vegetables to a warm plate.

COOK'S TIP
Use a firm but not hard cheese, such as Double Gloucester or Monterey Jack.

3 Wipe the pan with kitchen paper, then add the remaining oil and heat until really hot. Return the vegetables to the pan. Sprinkle the cheese over the top and season.

4 Pour in the beaten egg, making sure that it seeps under the vegetables. Cook over a low heat, stirring, until set. Serve hot or cold, in wedges, with the salsa. Garnish with fresh herbs and chilli.

CHEESE AND LEEK SAUSAGES WITH CHILLI AND TOMATO SAUCE

A SPICY SAUCE, MADE USING FRESH OR DRIED CHILLI AND FLAVOURED WITH BALSAMIC OR RED WINE VINEGAR, PEPS UP THESE POPULAR VEGETARIAN SAUSAGES.

SERVES FOUR

INGREDIENTS
  25g/1oz/2 tbsp butter
  175g/6oz leeks, finely chopped
  90ml/6 tbsp cold mashed potato
  115g/4oz/2 cups fresh
    white breadcrumbs
  150g/5oz/1¼ cups grated
    Caerphilly, Lancashire or
    Cantal cheese
  30ml/2 tbsp chopped fresh parsley
  5ml/1 tsp chopped fresh sage
    or marjoram
  2 large (US extra large) eggs, beaten
  good pinch of cayenne pepper
  65g/2½oz/scant 1 cup dry
    white breadcrumbs
  oil, for shallow frying
  salt and ground black pepper
For the sauce
  30ml/2 tbsp olive oil
  2 garlic cloves, thinly sliced
  1 fresh red chilli, seeded and finely
    chopped, or a good pinch of dried
    red chilli flakes
  1 small onion, finely chopped
  500g/1¼lb tomatoes, peeled, seeded
    and chopped
  a few fresh thyme sprigs
  10ml/2 tsp balsamic vinegar or red
    wine vinegar
  pinch of light muscovado
    (brown) sugar
  15–30ml/1–2 tbsp chopped fresh
    marjoram or oregano

1 Melt the butter in a pan and fry the leeks for 4–5 minutes, until softened but not browned. Mix with the mashed potato, fresh breadcrumbs, cheese, parsley and sage or marjoram. Add sufficient beaten egg (about two-thirds of the quantity) to bind the mixture. Season well and add the cayenne pepper to taste.

COOK'S TIP
These sausages are also delicious when they are served with chilli jam or a fruity chilli salsa.

2 Pat or roll the mixture between dampened hands to form 12 sausage shapes. Dip in the remaining egg, then coat in the dry breadcrumbs. Chill the coated sausages.

3 Make the sauce. Heat the oil in a pan and cook the garlic, chilli and onion over a low heat for 3–4 minutes. Add the tomatoes, thyme and vinegar. Season with salt, pepper and sugar.

4 Cook the sauce for 40–50 minutes, until considerably reduced. Remove the thyme and purée the sauce in a food processor or blender. Reheat with the marjoram or oregano and then adjust the seasoning.

5 Fry the sausages in shallow oil until golden brown on all sides. Drain on kitchen paper and serve with the sauce.

THAI MIXED VEGETABLE CURRY WITH LEMON GRASS RICE

FRAGRANT JASMINE RICE, SUBTLY FLAVOURED WITH LEMON GRASS AND CARDAMOM, IS THE PERFECT ACCOMPANIMENT TO THIS VEGETABLE CURRY.

SERVES FOUR

INGREDIENTS
- 10ml/2 tsp vegetable oil
- 400ml/14fl oz/1⅔ cups coconut milk
- 300ml/½ pint/1¼ cups vegetable stock
- 225g/8oz new potatoes, halved or quartered if large
- 130g/4½oz baby corn cobs
- 5ml/1 tsp granulated sugar
- 185g/6½oz/generous 1 cup broccoli florets
- 1 red (bell) pepper, seeded and sliced lengthways
- 115g/4oz spinach, tough stalks removed, leaves shredded
- 30ml/2 tbsp chopped fresh coriander (cilantro)
- salt and ground black pepper

For the spice paste
- 1 fresh red chilli, seeded and roughly chopped
- 3 fresh green chillies, seeded and roughly chopped
- 1 lemon grass stalk, outer layers removed and lower 5cm/2in chopped
- 2 shallots, chopped
- finely grated rind of 1 lime
- 2 garlic cloves, chopped
- 5ml/1 tsp ground coriander
- 2.5ml/½ tsp ground cumin
- 1cm/½in fresh galangal, chopped (optional)
- 30ml/2 tbsp chopped fresh coriander (cilantro)

For the rice
- 225g/8oz/generous 1 cup jasmine rice, rinsed and drained
- 1 lemon grass stalk, outer leaves removed, cut into 3 pieces
- 6 cardamom pods, bruised
- 475ml/16fl oz/2 cups water

1 Make the spice paste by grinding all the ingredients to a coarse paste in a food processor or blender. Scrape the paste out of the food processor or blender into a bowl, using a plastic spatula.

2 Heat the oil in a large heavy pan and fry the spice paste for 1–2 minutes, stirring constantly.

3 Pour in the coconut milk and stock, stir well and bring to the boil. Reduce the heat, add the potatoes and simmer for 15 minutes.

4 Meanwhile, prepare the rice. Tip the rice into a large pan and add the lemon grass and cardamom pods. Pour over the measured water.

COOK'S TIP
Save preparation time by making the spice paste the day before it is required. Cover and keep in the refrigerator.

5 Bring to the boil, then reduce the heat, cover, and cook for 10–15 minutes until the water has been absorbed and the rice is tender and slightly sticky. Season with salt, and leave to stand, covered, for 10 minutes.

6 Add the baby corn to the potatoes in the pan, with salt and pepper to taste, and cook for 2 minutes. Stir in the sugar, broccoli and red pepper, and cook for 2 minutes or until the vegetables are tender. Stir in the shredded spinach and half the fresh coriander. Cook for 2 minutes.

7 Remove the whole spices from the rice, fluff up the grains with a fork, then spoon into heated bowls. Top with the curry, sprinkled with the remaining fresh coriander.

VARIATIONS
- Substitute Thai aubergines (eggplant) for the potatoes.
- Use baby carrots instead of corn cobs.
- For non-vegetarians, add cooked prawns (shrimp) and just heat through.
- For protein, add toasted cashew nuts.

EGG AND GREEN LENTIL CURRY WITH GREEN CHILLIES AND GINGER

This simple and nourishing curry can be cooked in under an hour, from ingredients you may well have in your refrigerator or pantry. Serve the dish with your favourite chutney.

2 Boil the eggs for 10 minutes, then plunge them straight into cold water. When cool enough to handle, shell them and cut them in half lengthways.

3 Heat the oil in a large frying pan and fry the cloves and peppercorns for 2 minutes. Stir in the onion, chillies, garlic and ginger, and fry for a further 5–6 minutes, stirring frequently.

4 Stir in the curry paste and fry for a further 2 minutes, stirring constantly. Add the chopped tomatoes, sugar and water. Simmer for about 5 minutes until the sauce thickens, stirring occasionally. Add the boiled eggs, drained lentils and garam masala. Cover and simmer for 10 minutes, then serve.

COOK'S TIPS
• If you haven't got any fresh chillies, substitute dried ones. Reconstitute them by soaking in hot water for at least 20 minutes.
• A little sugar is often added to chillies, to soften the flavour. If you have any, try stirring in a spoonful of chilli jam instead, or a dash of Tabasco sauce.

SERVES FOUR

INGREDIENTS
    75g/3oz/scant ½ cup green lentils
    750ml/1¼ pints/3 cups stock
    6 eggs
    30ml/2 tbsp oil
    3 cloves
    1.5ml/¼ tsp black peppercorns
    1 onion, finely chopped
    2 fresh green chillies, finely chopped
    2 garlic cloves, crushed
    2.5cm/1in piece fresh root ginger,
      peeled and chopped
    30ml/2 tbsp curry paste
    400g/14oz can chopped tomatoes
    2.5ml/½ tsp granulated sugar
    175ml/6fl oz/¾ cup water
    2.5ml/½ tsp garam masala

1 Wash the lentils thoroughly under cold running water. Drain and check for small stones. Put the lentils in a large, heavy pan. Pour in the stock. Bring to the boil, then reduce the heat, cover and simmer gently for about 15 minutes or until the lentils are soft. Drain and set aside.

LENTIL DHAL <u>WITH</u> CHILLIES <u>AND</u> ROASTED GARLIC

FRESH AND DRIED CHILLIES FEATURE IN THIS SPICY LENTIL DHAL, WHICH MAKES A COMFORTING, STARCHY MEAL WHEN SERVED WITH BOILED RICE OR INDIAN BREADS.

SERVES FOUR TO SIX

INGREDIENTS

40g/1½oz/3 tbsp butter or ghee
1 onion, chopped
2 fresh green chillies, seeded
  and chopped
15ml/1 tbsp chopped fresh
  root ginger
225g/8oz/1 cup yellow or red lentils
900ml/1½ pints/3¾ cups water
1 head of garlic
5ml/1 tsp ground cumin
5ml/1 tsp ground coriander
2 tomatoes, peeled and diced
a little lemon juice
salt and ground black pepper
30–45ml/2–3 tbsp fresh coriander
  (cilantro) sprigs, to garnish
For the whole spice mix
30ml/2 tbsp groundnut (peanut) oil
4–5 shallots, sliced
2 garlic cloves, thinly sliced
15g/½oz/1 tbsp butter or ghee
5ml/1 tsp cumin seeds
5ml/1 tsp mustard seeds
3–4 small dried red chillies
8–10 fresh curry leaves

1 Melt the butter or ghee in a large pan and gently cook the onion, chillies and ginger for 10 minutes, stirring the mixture occasionally until golden.

2 Stir in the lentils and water. Bring to the boil, then reduce the heat and partially cover the pan. Simmer, stirring occasionally, for 50–60 minutes, until the texture resembles that of a very thick soup.

3 Meanwhile, preheat the oven to 180°C/350°F/Gas 4. Put the whole head of garlic in a small baking dish and roast for 30–45 minutes until soft.

4 Slice the top off the head of garlic. Scoop the roasted flesh into the lentil mixture, then stir in the cumin and ground coriander. Cook for a further 10–15 minutes, stirring frequently. Stir in the tomatoes, then season the mixture, adding lemon juice to taste.

5 For the spice mix, heat the oil in a small, heavy pan and fry the shallots until crisp and browned. Add the garlic and cook, stirring, until it colours slightly. Remove with a slotted spoon and set aside.

6 Melt the butter or ghee in the same pan and fry the cumin and mustard seeds until the mustard seeds pop. Stir in the chillies, curry leaves and the shallot mixture, then swirl most of the hot mixture into the dhal. Season. Top with the remaining spice mixture, garnish with coriander sprigs and serve.

PARSNIPS AND CHICKPEAS IN A CHILLI PASTE

THE SWEET FLAVOUR OF PARSNIPS GOES VERY WELL WITH THE SPICES IN THIS INDIAN-STYLE VEGETABLE STEW. SERVE IT WITH PLAIN YOGURT AND OFFER INDIAN BREADS TO MOP UP THE SAUCE.

SERVES FOUR

INGREDIENTS

200g/7oz/scant 1 cup dried
  chickpeas, soaked overnight in cold
  water, then drained
7 garlic cloves, finely chopped
1 small onion, chopped
5cm/2in piece fresh root
  ginger, chopped
2 fresh green chillies, such as
  jalapeños or serranos, seeded and
  finely chopped
550ml/18fl oz/2½ cups water
60ml/4 tbsp groundnut (peanut) oil
5ml/1 tsp cumin seeds
10ml/2 tsp ground coriander seeds
5ml/1 tsp ground turmeric
2.5–5ml/½–1 tsp mild chilli powder
50g/2oz/½ cup cashew nuts, toasted
  and ground
250g/9oz tomatoes, peeled
  and chopped
900g/2lb parsnips, cut into chunks
5ml/1 tsp ground toasted
  cumin seeds
juice of ½–1 lime
salt and ground black pepper
To serve
  fresh coriander (cilantro) leaves
  a few cashew nuts, toasted

1 Put the chickpeas in a pan, cover with cold water and bring to the boil. Boil vigorously for 10 minutes, then reduce the heat so that the water boils steadily and cook for 1–1½ hours, or until tender. The cooking time will depend on how long the chickpeas have been stored.

2 Meanwhile, for the sauce, set 10ml/ 2 tsp of the garlic aside, and place the remainder in a food processor or blender. Add the onion, ginger and half the chillies. Pour in 75ml/5 tbsp of the water and process to a smooth paste.

COOK'S TIP

For a milder result, use Anaheim chillies and mild paprika instead of chilli powder.

3 Heat the oil in a large, deep frying pan and cook the cumin seeds for 30 seconds. Stir in the coriander seeds, turmeric, chilli powder and ground cashew nuts. Add the ginger and chilli paste and cook, stirring frequently, until the water begins to evaporate. Add the tomatoes and stir-fry until the mixture begins to turn red-brown in colour.

4 Drain the chickpeas and add them to the pan, with the parsnips and remaining water. Season with 5ml/1 tsp salt and plenty of black pepper. Bring to the boil, stir, then simmer, uncovered, for 15–20 minutes, until the parsnips are completely tender.

5 Reduce the liquid, if necessary, by boiling fiercely until the sauce is thick. Add the ground toasted cumin with lime juice to taste. Stir in the reserved garlic and chilli, and cook for a final 1–2 minutes. Sprinkle the coriander leaves and toasted cashew nuts over and serve immediately.

VARIATIONS

Substitute red kidney beans for chickpeas or use carrots and butter (lima) beans.

TOFU AND GREEN BEAN RED CURRY

THE CHILLIES ARE STIRRED INTO THIS CURRY JUST BEFORE SERVING, SO CHOOSE A VARIETY WHOSE HEAT WILL BE TOLERABLE TO ALL YOUR GUESTS, OR OFFER THE CHILLIES SEPARATELY.

SERVES FOUR TO SIX

INGREDIENTS
600ml/1 pint/2½ cups coconut milk
15ml/1 tbsp red curry paste
45ml/3 tbsp Thai fish sauce
  (*nam pla*)
10ml/2 tsp palm sugar or soft dark
  brown sugar
225g/8oz/3 cups button
  (white) mushrooms
115g/4oz green beans, trimmed
175g/6oz firm tofu, rinsed and
  cut into 2cm/¾in cubes
4 kaffir lime leaves, torn
2 fresh red chillies, seeded
  and sliced
coriander (cilantro) leaves, to garnish

3 Add the green beans and cubes of tofu, and simmer gently for a further 4–5 minutes.

4 Stir in the kaffir lime leaves and chillies. Serve garnished with the coriander leaves.

1 Pour about one-third of the coconut milk into a pan. Cook until it starts to separate and an oily sheen appears.

2 Add the red curry paste, fish sauce and sugar to the coconut milk. Mix together thoroughly, then stir in the mushrooms and cook for 1 minute. Stir in the rest of the coconut milk and bring back to the boil.

COOK'S TIP
Firm tofu is suitable for stir-frying, braising and poaching. You can keep it in the refrigerator for up to 5 days by changing the water daily.

VARIATION
This works equally well with aubergines (eggplant), cauliflower, broccoli, bamboo shoots or a mixture of vegetables.

If you're serving a plain, simply cooked main course, you can transform it into something truly memorable by the addition of an exciting vegetable accompaniment such as Potatoes with Aubergines and Chillies, Balti-style Vegetables with Cashew Nuts, or Five-spice Vegetable Noodles. A spicy salad can also add a kick to meat, fish or egg dishes, or try a substantial main course salad, such as Thai Shellfish Salad with Chilli Dressing and Frizzled Shallots, Thai Beef Salad, or Gado-gado with Peanut and Chilli Sauce.

Side Dishes
and Salads

COURGETTES <u>WITH</u> CHILLI SAUCE

CRUNCHY COATED COURGETTES ARE GREAT SERVED WITH A FIERY TOMATO SAUCE. VEGETARIANS WILL LIKE THIS AS A MAIN DISH; MEAT AND FISH EATERS WILL APPRECIATE IT AS AN ACCOMPANIMENT.

SERVES TWO

INGREDIENTS
  15ml/1 tbsp olive oil
  1 onion, finely chopped
  1 fresh red chilli, seeded and
    finely diced
  10ml/2 tsp hot chilli powder
  400g/14oz can chopped tomatoes
  1 vegetable stock (bouillon) cube
  60ml/4 tbsp hot water
  450g/1lb courgettes (zucchini)
  150ml/¼ pint/⅔ cup milk
  50g/2oz/½ cup plain
    (all-purpose) flour
  oil for deep-frying
  salt and ground black pepper
  fresh thyme sprigs, to garnish
To serve
  lettuce leaves
  watercress sprigs (optional)
  slices of seeded bread

1 Heat the oil in a pan and fry the onion for 2–3 minutes. Stir in the chilli and chilli powder, and cook for 30 seconds.

2 Add the tomatoes. Crumble in the stock cube and stir in the water. Season to taste, cover and cook for 10 minutes.

VARIATION
Substitute baby leaf spinach for the watercress sprigs.

3 Meanwhile, trim the courgettes and cut them into 5mm/¼in slices.

4 Pour the milk into a shallow dish and spread out the flour in another. Dip the courgette slices in the milk, then into the flour, until well coated.

5 Heat the oil for deep-frying to 180°C/ 350°F or until a cube of day-old bread, added to the oil, browns in 30–45 seconds. Add the courgettes in batches and deep-fry for 3–4 minutes until crisp. Drain on kitchen paper.

6 Mix the courgettes with the sauce and place on warmed plates. Garnish with thyme sprigs and serve with lettuce, watercress, if using, and seeded bread.

POTATOES <u>WITH</u> AUBERGINES <u>AND</u> CHILLIES

USING BABY POTATOES ADDS TO THE ATTRACTIVENESS OF THIS DISH. CHOOSE THE SMALLER VARIETY OF AUBERGINES TOO, AS THEY ARE FAR TASTIER THAN THE LARGE ONES.

SERVES FOUR

INGREDIENTS
  10–12 waxy baby potatoes
  6 small aubergines (eggplant)
  1 medium red (bell) pepper
  1 fresh red chilli
  15ml/1 tbsp corn oil
  2 medium onions, sliced
  4–6 curry leaves
  2.5ml/½ tsp kalonji seeds
  5ml/1 tsp crushed coriander seeds
  2.5ml/½ tsp cumin seeds
  5ml/1 tsp grated fresh
    root ginger
  5ml/1 tsp crushed garlic
  5ml/1 tsp crushed dried red chillies
  15ml/1 tbsp chopped fresh fenugreek
    leaves (see Cook's Tip)
  5ml/1 tsp chopped fresh
    coriander (cilantro)
  15ml/1 tbsp natural (plain) yogurt
  fresh coriander (cilantro) leaves,
    to garnish

1 Bring a pan of lightly salted water to the boil, add the baby potatoes and cook for 10–15 minutes until just soft. Drain and set aside.

2 Cut the aubergines into quarters, leaving the stems attached.

COOK'S TIPS
• Fresh fenugreek leaves, called *methi*, are widely used in Indian cooking, particularly with potatoes, spinach and yam. If you can't find fresh leaves, use dried, or increase the quantity of fresh coriander.
• Small aubergines, with their stem, are readily available from Asian grocers.

3 Cut the pepper in half, remove the seeds, then slice the flesh into strips. Slit the chilli and scrape out the seeds with a sharp knife. Chop the flesh finely.

4 Heat the oil in a wok or frying pan and fry the onions, pepper strips, chopped fresh chillies, curry leaves, kalonji seeds, crushed coriander seeds and cumin seeds until the onions are a soft golden brown. (You may need to be careful when frying the curry leaves and seeds because they spit, sizzle and pop.)

5 Mix in the ginger, garlic, crushed chillies and fenugreek, followed by the aubergines and potatoes. Cover with a lid. Lower the heat and cook for 5–7 minutes.

6 Remove the lid, stir in the fresh coriander, then swirl in the yogurt. Serve immediately, garnished with the coriander leaves.

COOK'S TIP
Curry leaves are small and almond-shaped. They can be found in Asian food stores.

BALTI-STYLE VEGETABLES WITH CASHEW NUTS

IT IS THE PREPARATION THAT TAKES THE TIME HERE. DO IT IN ADVANCE AND EVERYONE WILL BE IMPRESSED AT THE SPEED WITH WHICH YOU'LL BE ABLE TO PRODUCE A DELICIOUS MEAL.

SERVES FOUR

INGREDIENTS
  2 carrots
  1 red (bell) pepper, seeded
  1 green (bell) pepper, seeded
  2 courgettes (zucchini)
  115g/4oz green beans, trimmed
  1 medium bunch spring
    onions (scallions)
  15ml/1 tbsp extra virgin olive oil
  4–6 curry leaves
  2.5ml/½ tsp white cumin seeds
  4 dried red chillies
  10–12 cashew nuts
  5ml/1 tsp salt
  30ml/2 tbsp lemon juice
  fresh mint leaves, to garnish
  cooked rice, to serve (optional)

1 Prepare the vegetables: cut the carrots, peppers and courgettes into matchsticks, halve the beans and chop the spring onions. Set aside.

VARIATION
Use peanuts instead of cashew nuts, and baby leeks for spring onions.

2 Heat the oil in a wok or frying pan and fry the curry leaves, cumin seeds and dried chillies for about 1 minute, until aromatic. Be careful with the timing, as curry leaves quickly burn.

3 Add the vegetables and nuts, and stir-fry for 3–4 minutes. Add the salt and lemon juice. Toss the vegetables over the heat for 3–5 minutes more, until they are crisp-tender.

4 Lift out and discard the curry leaves. Spoon the fragrant stir-fry on to a heated serving dish and garnish with mint leaves. Serve immediately, with boiled rice, if you like.

BALTI URAD DHAL <u>WITH</u> GREEN <u>AND</u> RED CHILLIES

URAD DHAL, OFF-WHITE HULLED, SPLIT PEAS, IS JUST ONE OF MANY DIFFERENT PULSES SOLD IN INDIAN FOOD STORES. THE FLAVOUR IS ENLIVENED WHEN COOKED WITH CHILLIES AND OTHER SPICES.

2 Heat the oil in a wok or frying pan over a medium heat. Fry the bay leaf with the onions and cinnamon bark.

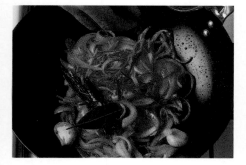

3 Add the ginger, whole garlic cloves and half the green and red chillies.

4 Drain almost all the water from the split peas. Add to the wok or frying pan, followed by the remaining green and red chillies and finally the fresh mint. Heat through briefly and serve.

COOK'S TIP
For a milder curry, replace some of the chillies with green or red (bell) peppers which will also add colour to the dish.

<u>SERVES FOUR</u>

INGREDIENTS
   115g/4oz/½ cup urad dhal or
     yellow split peas
   30ml/2 tbsp corn oil
   1 bay leaf
   2 onions, sliced
   1 piece cinnamon bark
   15ml/1 tbsp grated fresh
     root ginger
   2 garlic cloves
   2 fresh green chillies, seeded and
     sliced lengthways
   2 fresh red chillies, seeded and
     sliced lengthways
   15ml/1 tbsp chopped
     fresh mint

1 Put the dhal or split peas in a bowl and pour in enough cold water to cover by at least 2.5cm/1in. Cover and leave to soak overnight. Next day, drain the dhal and boil it in water until the individual grains are soft enough to break into two. Set aside.

CHILLI CHIVE RICE WITH MUSHROOMS

WHILE COOKING, THIS RICE DISH DEVELOPS A WONDERFUL AROMA, WHICH IS MATCHED BY THE COMPLEMENTARY FLAVOURS OF CHILLI, GARLIC CHIVES AND FRESH CORIANDER.

3 Add the rice to the onions and fry over a low heat, stirring frequently, for 4–5 minutes. Pour in the stock mixture, then stir in the salt and a good grinding of black pepper.

4 Bring to the boil, stir and reduce the heat to very low. Cover tightly and cook for 15–20 minutes, until the rice has absorbed all the liquid.

5 Remove from the heat. Lay a clean, folded dishtowel over the open pan and press on the lid, jamming it firmly in place. Leave to stand for 10 minutes. The towel will absorb the steam while the rice becomes completely tender.

6 Meanwhile, heat the remaining oil in a frying pan and cook the mushrooms for 5–6 minutes, until tender and browned. Add the remaining chives and cook for a further 1–2 minutes.

7 Stir the mixed, sliced mushrooms and chopped fresh coriander leaves into the cooked rice. Adjust the seasoning, transfer to a warmed serving dish and serve immediately, sprinkled with the cashew nuts.

SERVES FOUR

INGREDIENTS
- 350g/12oz/1¾ cups long grain rice
- 60ml/4 tbsp groundnut (peanut) oil
- 1 small onion, finely chopped
- 2 fresh green chillies, seeded and finely chopped
- a handful of garlic chives, chopped
- 15g/½oz/¼ cup fresh coriander (cilantro)
- 600ml/1 pint/2½ cups vegetable or mushroom stock
- 5ml/1 tsp salt
- 250g/9oz/3–3½ cups mixed mushrooms, thickly sliced
- 50g/2oz/½ cup cashew nuts, fried in 15ml/1 tbsp oil until golden brown
- ground black pepper

1 Wash and drain the rice. Heat half the oil in a pan and cook the onion and chillies over a low heat, stirring occasionally, for 10–12 minutes, until soft, but not browned.

2 Set half the garlic chives aside. Cut the stalks off the coriander and set the leaves aside. Purée the remaining chives and the coriander stalks with the stock in a blender or food processor.

COOK'S TIP
Wild mushrooms are often expensive, but they do have distinctive flavours. Mixing them with cultivated mushrooms is an economical way of using them. Look for ceps, chanterelles, oyster, morels and horse mushrooms.

MEXICAN RICE

CHILLIES PLAY A SUPPORTING ROLE IN THIS SIMPLE BUT DELICIOUS RECIPE. LEAVING THEM WHOLE LIMITS THEIR IMPACT, BUT STILL MAKES A CONTRIBUTION TO THE FINISHED DISH.

SERVES SIX

INGREDIENTS
  200g/7oz/1 cup long grain rice
  200g/7oz can chopped tomatoes in
    tomato juice
  ½ onion, roughly chopped
  2 garlic cloves, roughly chopped
  30ml/2 tbsp vegetable oil
  450ml/¾ pint/scant 2 cups
    vegetable stock
  2.5ml/½ tsp salt
  3 fresh green fresno chillies or other
    fresh green chillies
  150g/5oz/1 cup frozen peas
  ground black pepper

1 Put the rice in a large heatproof bowl and pour over boiling water to cover. Stir once, then leave to stand for 10 minutes. Drain, rinse under cold water, then drain again. Leave in the sieve and set aside to dry slightly.

2 Meanwhile, pour the tomatoes and juice into a food processor or blender, add the onion and garlic, and process until smooth.

3 Heat the oil in a large, heavy pan, add the rice and cook over a medium heat until it becomes a delicate golden brown. Stir occasionally to ensure that the rice does not stick to the base of the pan. Reduce the heat if the rice begins to darken too much.

4 Add the tomato mixture and stir over a medium heat until all the liquid has been absorbed. Stir in the stock, salt, whole chillies and peas.

5 Continue to cook the mixture, stirring occasionally, until all the liquid has been absorbed and the rice is just tender. Season with pepper.

6 Remove the pan from the heat, cover it with a tight-fitting lid and leave it to stand in a warm place for 5–10 minutes. Remove the chillies, fluff up the rice lightly and serve, sprinkled with black pepper. The chillies can be used as a garnish, if you like.

COOK'S TIP
Do not stir the rice too often after you add the stock or the grains will break down and the mixture will quickly become starchy.

FIVE-SPICE VEGETABLE NOODLES

THE MELLOW WARMTH OF FIVE-SPICE POWDER PROVIDES AN EXCELLENT COUNTERPOINT TO THE RAW HEAT OF THE CHILLIES IN THIS SUPERB STIR-FRY.

2 Cut the carrots and celery into matchstick strips. Cut the fennel bulb in half and cut out the hard core. Cut into slices, then cut the slices into matchstick strips.

3 Cut both chillies in half and scrape out the seeds with a sharp knife. Cut 1 chilli into slices and chop the remaining chilli finely.

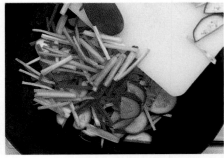

4 Heat the remaining oil in a wok until very hot. Add all the vegetables, with the chopped chilli, and stir-fry for about 7–8 minutes.

5 Add the ginger and garlic, and stir-fry for 2 minutes, then stir in the spices. Cook for 1 minute. Add the spring onions and stir-fry for 1 minute. Pour in the warm water and cook for 1 minute.

SERVES TWO TO THREE

INGREDIENTS
   225g/8oz dried egg noodles
   30ml/2 tbsp sesame oil
   2 carrots
   1 celery stick
   1 small fennel bulb
   2 fresh red chillies
   2 courgettes (zucchini), halved
     and sliced
   2.5cm/1in piece of fresh root ginger,
     peeled and grated
   1 garlic clove, crushed
   7.5ml/1½ tsp Chinese
     five-spice powder
   2.5ml/½ tsp ground cinnamon
   4 spring onions (scallions), sliced
   60ml/4 tbsp warm water

1 Bring a large pan of lightly salted water to the boil. Add the noodles and cook for 2–3 minutes until just tender. Drain the noodles thoroughly in a colander, return them to the pan and toss in a little of the oil. Set aside. Tossing them in oil in this way will keep them from sticking together as they cool.

6 Stir in the noodles and toss over the heat until the noodles have heated through. Serve sprinkled with the sliced red chilli.

COOK'S TIP
A cleaver is the preferred cutting tool used in Chinese cooking.

GADO-GADO <u>WITH</u> PEANUT <u>AND</u> CHILLI SAUCE

A BANANA LEAF, WHICH CAN BE BOUGHT FROM ASIAN FOOD STORES, CAN BE USED AS WELL AS THE MIXED SALAD LEAVES TO LINE THE PLATTER FOR A SPECIAL OCCASION.

SERVES SIX

INGREDIENTS
½ cucumber
2 pears (not too ripe) or 175g/6oz
   wedge of yam bean (jicama)
1–2 eating apples
juice of ½ lemon
mixed salad leaves
6 small tomatoes, cut in wedges
3 slices fresh pineapple, cored and
   cut in wedges
3 eggs, hard-boiled, shelled and
   sliced or quartered
175g/6oz egg noodles, cooked,
   cooled and chopped
deep-fried onions, to garnish
For the peanut sauce
2–4 fresh red chillies, seeded
   and ground, or 15ml/1 tbsp
   chilli sambal
300ml/½ pint/1¼ cups coconut milk
350g/12oz/1¼ cups crunchy
   peanut butter
15ml/1 tbsp dark soy sauce or soft
   dark brown sugar
5ml/1 tsp tamarind pulp, soaked in
   45ml/3 tbsp warm water
coarsely crushed peanuts
salt

2 Simmer gently until the sauce thickens, then stir in the soy sauce or sugar. Strain in the tamarind juice, add salt to taste and stir well. Spoon into a bowl and sprinkle with a few coarsely crushed peanuts.

VARIATION
Quail's eggs can be used instead of hen's eggs and look very attractive in this dish. Hard-boil for 3 minutes, shell, then halve or leave whole.

3 To make the salad, core the cucumber and peel the pears or yam bean. Cut them into matchsticks. Finely shred the apples and sprinkle them with the lemon juice. Spread a bed of salad leaves on a flat platter, then pile the fruit and vegetables on top.

4 Add the sliced or quartered hard-boiled eggs, the chopped noodles and the deep-fried onions. Serve immediately, with the sauce.

1 Make the peanut sauce. Put the chillies or chilli sambal in a pan. Pour in the coconut milk. Stir in the peanut butter. Heat gently, stirring, until mixed.

COOK'S TIP
To make your own peanut butter, process roasted peanuts in a food processor, slowly adding vegetable oil to achieve the right texture. Add salt to taste.

PINK AND GREEN SALAD

THERE'S JUST ENOUGH CHILLI IN THIS STUNNING SALAD TO BRING A ROSY BLUSH TO YOUR CHEEKS.

SERVES FOUR

INGREDIENTS
225g/8oz/2 cups dried farfalle or
  other pasta shapes
juice of ½ lemon
1 small fresh red chilli, seeded and
  very finely chopped
60ml/4 tbsp chopped fresh basil
30ml/2 tbsp chopped fresh
  coriander (cilantro)
60ml/4 tbsp extra virgin olive oil
15ml/1 tbsp mayonnaise
250g/9oz peeled cooked
  prawns (shrimp)
1 avocado
salt and ground black pepper

1 Bring a large pan of lightly salted water to the boil and cook the pasta for 10–12 minutes, folllowing the packet instructions, or until it is *al dente*.

2 Meanwhile, put the lemon juice and chilli in a bowl with half the basil and coriander. Add salt and pepper to taste. Whisk well to mix, then whisk in the oil and mayonnaise until thick. Add the prawns and stir to coat in the dressing.

3 Drain the pasta in a colander, and rinse under cold running water until cold. Leave to drain and dry, shaking the colander occasionally.

4 Halve, stone (pit) and peel the avocado, then cut the flesh into dice. Add to the prawns and dressing with the pasta, toss well to mix and taste for seasoning. Serve immediately, sprinkled with the remaining basil and coriander.

COOK'S TIP
Keep a few chillies in the freezer and you'll never need to worry about getting fresh supplies just when you want them.

COUSCOUS AND CHILLI SALAD

THIS IS A SPICY VARIATION ON A CLASSIC TABBOULEH, TRADITIONALLY MADE WITH BULGUR WHEAT AND NOT COUSCOUS, WHICH IS ACTUALLY A FORM OF SEMOLINA GRAIN.

SERVES FOUR

INGREDIENTS

   45ml/3 tbsp olive oil
   5 spring onions (scallions), chopped
   1 garlic clove, crushed
   5ml/1 tsp ground cumin
   350ml/12fl oz/1½ cups
     vegetable stock
   175g/6oz/1 cup couscous
   2 tomatoes, peeled and chopped
   60ml/4 tbsp chopped fresh parsley
   60ml/4 tbsp chopped fresh mint
   1 fresh green chilli, seeded and
     finely chopped
   30ml/2 tbsp lemon juice
   salt and ground black pepper
   crisp lettuce leaves, to serve
   toasted pine nuts and grated lemon
     rind, to garnish

1 Heat the oil in a pan. Add the spring onions and garlic. Stir in the cumin and cook over a medium heat for 1 minute. Pour in the stock and bring to the boil.

2 Remove the pan from the heat, stir in the couscous, cover the pan tightly and leave to stand for 10 minutes, until all the liquid has been absorbed.

3 Tip the couscous into a bowl. Stir in the tomatoes, parsley, mint, chilli and lemon juice, and season. Leave to stand for 1 hour for the flavours to develop.

4 To serve, line a bowl with lettuce leaves and spoon the couscous salad into the centre. Sprinkle toasted pine nuts and lemon rind over, to garnish.

VARIATIONS
• You can use fine bulgur wheat instead of couscous. Follow the packet instructions for its preparation.
• It is very important for the flavour of the salad to use fresh mint. If it is not available, substitute fresh coriander. The flavour will not be quite the same but dried or freeze-dried mint are not suitable alternatives.

THAI SHELLFISH SALAD <u>WITH</u> CHILLI DRESSING <u>AND</u> FRIZZLED SHALLOTS

IN THIS INTENSELY FLAVOURED SALAD, SWEET PRAWNS AND MANGO ARE PARTNERED WITH A SWEET-SOUR GARLIC DRESSING HEIGHTENED WITH THE HOT TASTE OF CHILLI.

SERVES FOUR TO SIX

INGREDIENTS
  675g/1½lb raw prawns (shrimp),
    shelled and deveined, with
    tails on
  finely shredded rind of 1 lime
  ½ fresh red chilli, seeded and
    finely chopped
  30ml/2 tbsp olive oil, plus extra
    for brushing
  1 ripe but firm mango
  2 carrots, cut into long
    thin shreds
  10cm/4in piece cucumber, sliced
  1 small red onion, halved and
    thinly sliced
  45ml/3 tbsp roasted peanuts,
    roughly chopped
  salt and ground black pepper
For the dressing
  1 large garlic clove, chopped
  10–15ml/2–3 tsp granulated sugar
  juice of 1½–2 limes
  15–30ml/1–2 tbsp Thai fish sauce
    (*nam pla*)
  1 fresh red chilli, seeded
  5–10ml/1–2 tsp light rice vinegar
For the frizzled shallots
  30ml/2 tbsp groundnut
    (peanut) oil
  4 large shallots, thinly sliced

COOK'S TIPS
• Crisp frizzled shallots are a traditional addition to Thai salads.
• For an authentic flavour, use Pacific shrimp, which are a wonderful brownish blue when raw. If they are frozen, make sure they are thawed before using.
• When searing the prawns, make sure that they have all turned pink, as undercooked prawns are unpleasant to eat and may be harmful. However, do not overcook, which spoils the texture.
• Mangoes vary considerably. Some are ripe when the skin is green flushed with red; others when they are red-gold or yellow. Ripe mangoes give gently when squeezed lightly in the palm of the hand.

1 Place the prawns in a glass or china dish and add the lime rind and chilli. Season with salt and pepper, and spoon the oil over. Toss to mix, cover and leave to marinate for 30–40 minutes.

2 Make the dressing. Place the garlic in a mortar with 10ml/2 tsp sugar. Pound until smooth, then work in the juice of 1½ limes and 15ml/1 tbsp of the fish sauce.

3 Transfer the dressing to a jug (pitcher). Finely chop half the fresh red chilli, and add it to the dressing. Taste the mixture and add more sugar, lime juice, fish sauce and the rice vinegar to taste.

4 Cut through the mango lengthwise 1cm/½in from each side of the centre to free the stone (pit). Remove all the peel and cut the flesh away from the stone. Cut all the flesh into fine strips. Set the mango aside. Make the frizzled shallots by heating the oil in a wok or frying pan and frying them until crisp. Drain on kitchen paper and set aside.

5 In a bowl, toss the mango, carrots, cucumber and onion with half the dressing. Arrange the salad on individual plates or in bowls.

6 Heat a ridged, cast-iron griddle pan or heavy frying pan until very hot. Brush the prawns with a little oil, then sear them for 2–3 minutes on each side, until they turn pink and are patched with brown on the outside. Arrange the prawns on the salads.

7 Sprinkle the remaining dressing over the salads. Finely shred the remaining chilli and sprinkle it over the salads with the crisp-fried shallots. Serve, with the peanuts handed around separately.

VARIATIONS
• Use scallops or chicken breast portions instead of prawns.
• Chop cashew nuts in place of peanuts.
• Substitute finely sliced baby leeks for the shallots.
• Make into a more substantial meal by mixing with cooked pasta shapes.

LARP OF CHIANG MAI

ANYONE WHO HAS TRAVELLED THROUGH NORTH-EASTERN THAILAND IS LIKELY TO HAVE ENCOUNTERED THIS TRADITIONAL DISH, IN WHICH CHICKEN IS COATED IN A HOT AND SHARP CHILLI SAUCE.

SERVES FOUR TO SIX

INGREDIENTS
  450g/1lb minced (ground) chicken
  1 lemon grass stalk, trimmed
  3 kaffir lime leaves, finely chopped
  4 fresh red chillies, seeded
    and chopped
  60ml/4 tbsp lime juice
  30ml/2 tbsp Thai fish sauce
    (*nam pla*)
  15ml/1 tbsp roasted ground rice
    (see Cook's Tip)
  2 spring onions (scallions), chopped
  30ml/2 tbsp fresh coriander
    (cilantro) leaves
  thinly sliced kaffir lime leaves, mixed
    salad leaves and fresh mint sprigs,
    to garnish

1 Heat a large non-stick frying pan. Add the chicken and moisten with a little water. Stir constantly over a medium heat for 7–10 minutes until it is cooked.

2 While the chicken is cooking, cut off the lower 5cm/2in of the lemon grass stalk and chop finely.

3 Transfer the cooked chicken to a bowl and add the chopped lemon grass, lime leaves, chillies, lime juice, fish sauce, ground rice, spring onions and coriander leaves. Mix thoroughly.

4 Spoon the chicken mixture into a salad bowl. Sprinkle sliced kaffir lime leaves over the top and garnish with salad leaves and sprigs of mint.

COOK'S TIP
Use glutinous rice (a short to medium grain rice) for the roasted ground rice. Put in a frying pan and dry-roast it until golden brown. Remove and grind to a powder, using a mortar and pestle or a food processor. When the rice is cold, store it in a glass jar in a cool, dry place.

THAI BEEF SALAD

A HEARTY MAIN MEAL SALAD, THIS COMBINES TENDER STRIPS OF STEAK WITH A WONDERFUL CHILLI AND LIME DRESSING. SERVE IT WITH WARM CRUSTY BREAD OR A BOWL OF RICE.

SERVES FOUR

INGREDIENTS
  oil, for frying
  2 sirloin steaks, each
    about 225g/8oz
  1 lemon grass stalk, trimmed
  1 red onion, finely sliced
  ½–1 fresh red chilli,
    finely chopped
  ½ cucumber, cut into strips
  30ml/2 tbsp chopped spring
    onion (scallion)
  juice of 2 limes
  15–30ml/1–2 tbsp Thai fish sauce
    (*nam pla*)
  Chinese mustard cress, or fresh
    herbs, to garnish

COOK'S TIP
Look out for gui chai leaves in Thai groceries. These look like very thin spring onions and are often used as a substitute for the more familiar vegetable.

1 Heat a large frying pan until hot, add a little oil and pan-fry the steaks for 6–8 minutes for medium-rare. If you prefer, cook the steaks under a preheated medium grill (broiler). Allow to rest for 10–15 minutes.

2 Cut off the lower 5cm/2in of the lemon grass stalk and chop it finely.

3 When the meat is cool, slice it thinly on a cutting board and put the slices in a large bowl.

4 Add the sliced onion, chilli, cucumber, lemon grass and chopped spring onion to the meat slices.

5 Toss the salad and flavour with the lime juice and fish sauce. Transfer to a serving bowl or plate and serve at room temperature or chilled, garnished with Chinese mustard cress or fresh herbs.

VARIATION
Instead of beef, use pork, chicken or meaty tuna steaks.

INDEX

ACKNOWLEDGEMENTS
The consultant editor,
Jenni Fleetwood,
would like to thank
Christine McFadden,
Michael Michaud, and
fellow members of the
Guild of Food Writers,
for sharing their
knowledge of and
enthusiasm for chillies.
    Michael and Joy
Michaud are market
gardeners, and from
July to December
each year they can
supply fresh chillies
by mail order. Contact
them at Peppers by
Post, Sea Spring
Farm, West Bexington,
Dorchester, Dorset
DT2 9DD, UK,
tel: 01308 897892